C000229235

A Schoolboy's
War
in Cornwall

A SCHOOLBOY'S WAR IN CORNWALL

JIM REEVE

The History Press

First published 2010

The History Press
The Mill, Brimscombe Port
Stroud, Gloucestershire, GL5 2QG
www.thehistorypress.co.uk

© Jim Reeve, 2010

The right of Jim Reeve to be identified as the Author
of this work has been asserted in accordance with the
Copyrights, Designs and Patents Act 1988.

All rights reserved. No part of this book may be reprinted
or reproduced or utilised in any form or by any electronic,
mechanical or other means, now known or hereafter invented,
including photocopying and recording, or in any information
storage or retrieval system, without the permission in writing
from the Publishers.

British Library Cataloguing in Publication Data.
A catalogue record for this book is available from the British Library.

ISBN 978 0 7524 5540 2
Typesetting and origination by The History Press
Printed in Great Britain
Manufacturing managed by Jellyfish Print Solutions Ltd

Contents

ACKNOWLEDGEMENTS

I would like to thank the many people who have assisted me in compiling this book and who have generously given me their time, shared their evacuation experiences and loaned me their precious photographs. I would especially like to thank Jim Wright of the Evacuees Reunion Association, who has been so helpful in supplying photographs and information; the editor of the *West Briton*, Richard Vanhinsbergh, for printing my letter in the paper, to which I had so many replies; the staff of the Redruth Library; the staff of the Truro Museum; Angela Broome, BA (Hons), at the Courtney Library Cornish History Research Centre; Steve Perry at his excellent Cornwall at War Museum in Davidstow, a museum not to be missed on any visit to Cornwall; Mr and Mrs May at the Great Western Hotel; Mr Cooley and Mr Stephen Smith at the Atlantic Hotel, who were so helpful; the voluntary staff at the Maritime Museum, Falmouth, and, in the order I interviewed them, Mrs F. Bishop; John Glyn; Eileen Penwarden; Roger and Wendy Watson; Madeline Fereday; Professor Ken MacKinnon; Edna Goreing; Dave Thomson; Mrs Sheila Nicholls; Mrs Jones; Ken Foxon; Yvonne Watson; Stan Mason; Sheila Sells; Harry Drury; Mrs Murt; Mary Garnham; Brian Little; Mrs J. Harris; Mr Clark; Mr R.A. Cook; Mrs Jean Pickering (née Desforges), who represented Great Britain in the 1952 Olympic Games; Mr Wills; Nancy Botterell; Ian Blackwell; Clive Mathison; Anne Vaughan; Elsie and Rose Bristol, Mrs Pellew (née Gribble); Mrs M. Pascoe; the three Horton sisters, Betty, Irene, and Olive; Peter Butt; John Reid; Mr Shire; Michael Duhig; Olive West; Mr and Mrs Trip; and Mrs Patricia Free (née Wood). Also, my gratitude goes to my editors, Sophie Bradshaw, Nicola Guy and David Lewis; my researcher and good friend Olive Norfolk; my wife, Joan, for her help, support, understanding and editing skills and, finally, to all the people who took us in during those turbulent times.

INTRODUCTION

It is important to record the wartime experiences of ordinary children who were evacuated before their memories are lost in the mists of time. This book sets out to log the experiences of children, often as young as four years old, who were evacuated from the danger zones that were targeted by the German Air Force. Many readers may disagree with some of the facts mentioned, but these are the memories of people as they recalled them, and one should bear in mind that the events took place over seventy years ago.

During the First World War, towns were bombed by the German Zeppelins and Gotha bombers and therefore it was realized that as we slipped reluctantly towards the Second World War, a scheme of evacuation had to be planned. As Stanley Baldwin MP said, 'The bomber will always get through.' As far back as 1931, a sub-committee was set up to examine the problem of evacuating the young and vulnerable away from the danger areas. The plans were well advanced by the time Chamberlain made his famous remark of 'peace for our time' from the window of 10 Downing Street after returning from Munich and giving his famous speech on the steps of the Lockheed plane at Heston Airfield in September 1938.

The government took measures under the Emergency Powers Act in August 1939 which enabled them to commandeer houses, restrict menus to one item, close theatres and cinemas and force factories to manufacture whatever was needed for the war effort to ensure victory. From 1 September, and for the next few days, 3,000 buses were commandeered, routes along main roads were changed to one way only and 4,000 trains took the children to safe parts of the country. The evacuees were not told where they were going, which created an air of excitement and anticipation. There were 1,200 helpers but everyone at the stations became involved; policemen carried cases and porters helped mothers with young children as everyone had a single purpose in mind: to get the children safely away. Whole schools were evacuated with their teachers but parents were not allowed to see their children off and stood outside the playgrounds in tears. The streets were alive with 1½ million children from every bomb-threatened area in the country. All of them carried a gas mask and food for the day. Their names were attached to their lapels. The declaration of the Second World War was two days away, but the invasion of Poland on 1 September 1939 triggered 'Operation Pied Piper' and the great evacuation began. I remember it well!

When the children finally arrived at their place of safety, exhausted after their journey, they were lined up in village halls, schools and even sometimes on the station platform, where the foster parents picked out the ones they wanted. This often meant splitting up brothers and sisters. The badly dressed children from the poorer districts of the cities were often left till last. One woman, who is in her late seventies, commented, 'It was like a slave market as I stood there waiting to be selected.' The foster parents were paid 10s 6d per week for the first child and 8s 6d for further children. Householders who provided lodgings for mothers with children under school age were paid 5s per week, but the mothers had to provide their own food, etc.

Most children were treated well and many formed friendships which have lasted to this day, but to others the evacuation was a nightmare. Mrs Willingham from Bethnal Green, who was evacuated to Cornwall, had an appalling time and finished up being thrown down the stairs. She was bathed in cold water, even in the depths of winter. Some local children resented the evacuees and fights broke out. Evacuees often came from different backgrounds to those who fostered them; children from the slums were billeted with middle-class families who had no concept of what hardship was. Some children were so poor that they arrived without a change of clothes and their foster parents had to go out and buy new ones.

Inevitably, with vast numbers of people on the move, there were many mistakes. In some villages too many children arrived, giving billeting officers a headache in finding them places, while in others, the opposite happened. In fact, it was reported that some villages on the Yorkshire Moors turned out to welcome the evacuees in force but many of the villagers returned home disappointed because there were not enough children to go round. It is amazing that of all the children that were evacuated there was only one fatality; Michael Moscow, who came from London and was billeted in Market Harborough, was shot dead by his brother while they were playing with a shotgun.

The Minister of Health, Mr Walter Elliot, described the evacuation as the equivalent to moving ten armies. It was not compulsory and many parents were unwilling to part with their children. Of those that did go, 90,000 returned home within a short while because the expected bombing did not happen, but when the Blitz did start in earnest in 1940 there was another great exodus from the cities.

My mother was determined that Hitler was not going to drive her out of her home but quickly changed her mind when a bomb wrecked our house in 1940. Because my brother was a baby, my mother accompanied us and we finished up in the very classy Great Western Hotel in Newquay, Cornwall, which for me was a great adventure. Many children went to Canada, America and Australia but, sadly, the SS *City of Benares*, which was bound for Canada with ninety children on board, was torpedoed by the German U-boat *U-48* and sank. Only thirteen children were saved by HMS *Anthony*, 500 miles off the north-west coast of Ireland, on 17 September 1940.

To celebrate the seventieth anniversary of the start of the evacuation, the Evacuees Reunion Association held a service in St Paul's Cathedral on 1 September 2009, where approximately 2,000 evacuees gave their thanks for having come through the journey into the unknown.

Jim Reeve
September 2010

I

WAR IS DECLARED

The day before Hitler invaded Poland, the final of three warnings went out to 'Evacuate Forthwith'. Mothers and families who lived in a region designated as an evacuation area, and who had volunteered to send their children to a reception area, began to say their goodbyes. For a while, children had gone to school with their gas masks, enough food for the day and carrying clothing, according to instructions that had been sent out by the schools on orders of the government, who did not know when the order to 'Evacuate Forthwith' would come. The only person in the schools who knew the destination of the children was the headmaster and he was sworn to secrecy. Parents did not know where their sons or daughters were until they received a postcard from their child once they had arrived at their destination.

At first it was decided that children should go with their schools, but given one child from a family could go to a senior school and another to a junior school, it was soon realized that they would be split up. There was such an uproar that the government soon changed its mind and children from the same family went together, although many were often separated when they reached their destinations.

Children were not the only ones evacuated. Mothers with children under school age, pregnant women and invalids also left and a number of hospitals were emptied out. Many evacuees were lucky enough to be sent to Cornwall and set out in this chapter are some of their experiences of how their parents came to make the decision to send them away to safety.

The first evacuation, which started on the 1 September 1939, was well organised considering the number of people involved but, to a certain extent, was a waste of time and money because the expected bombing of the cities did not take place. There was some bombing of ports and shipping but not towns. In view of this, parents began to believe that the government had exaggerated the risk and had got it wrong and it is estimated that 90,000 children returned home.

My mother had made up her mind that the war was not going to force her to leave home and so she decided not to have me or my brother Billy evacuated when the war started on 3 September 1939, until her mind was changed one night a year later after the Blitz had started in earnest. We lay on a mattress on the basement floor, under an old, wooden kitchen table, listening to the symphony of death as bombs cascaded out of the night sky onto London. Mum spread herself across us like a broody hen, gathering us beneath her great frame. Terrified, my Aunt Milly curled up beside us uttering, 'Oh my God, that was close. Lou, you must get the kids inoculated.'

'You mean evacuated, don't you?' Milly always got things wrong and Mum was always correcting her. Another bomb exploded and I remember snuggling closer to Mum. Suddenly our whole world seemed to implode and chunks of glass flew across the room. Lumps of plaster crashed to the ground, sending up clouds of dust. To add to the chaos, Billy started screaming.

Mothers were urged to evacuate their children.

In July 1940, as we lay there under the table with Billy yelling in my ear, I was terrified and then, suddenly, a loud noise penetrated the air in one long, continuous note, a sound we would welcome each time we heard it, for it would mean we had survived another enemy raid. Very carefully, we crawled out of our sanctuary, trying to avoid the glass which was scattered across the floor. Mum carried Billy in her arms while Aunt Milly took my hand and led me up the stairs. I remember looking up and, to my surprise, seeing the sky and wondering why? Then I realized the front door was hanging off at an angle and clinging to the frame by one hinge. Just as we reached the top of the stairs I saw a helmet poke over the limp door with ARW (air raid warden) painted in white on it. In a cheerful voice he shouted, 'You alright down there?' and with one accord we shouted back 'Yes!'

The air was filled with dust as we stepped over the rubble and glass and carefully climbed the stairs. Our house had three bedrooms. Mum and Dad had one, Billy and I had another and the third was used as a storage room. Mum stepped into ours and screamed. Looking round Mum, I saw daylight where our window had been. 'Look, look at Jimmy's bed. Thank God he wasn't in it!'

My heart missed a beat as I saw a great window lintel lying across my bed. Had I been in it, I would have been killed. Mum was still carrying Billy on one arm but with the other she encircled me and pulled me to her. With her great arm around me all the fear of the previous night vanished. She always had that power to make me feel safe. The other rooms had not suffered as much, although the windows were out; it might have been that our room was at the front of the house. We discovered later that a bomb had fallen a little way up the road. When we went into the kitchen, we were surprised to find it had hardly been touched. Mum sat down and said, 'Let's have a cup of tea, I think it's safe. I can't smell gas.' So we sat in the kitchen drinking strong, hot, sweet tea, which seemed to be the cure for all the ills of the world in those far-off days.

We all started to clear up the mess except Billy, who was left in the playpen in the kitchen with his favourite teddy bear. I was warned to mind the glass but I suspect I was more of a hindrance than anything else. That afternoon some men came round and boarded up the windows and made some temporary repairs to the damage in our room and declared that the house was safe. They promised they would be back when they had some glass. To my knowledge, we never saw them again as I can remember how dark it was until we were evacuated.

While I drank my tea I thought back to how it had all begun. I did not understand this talk of war. The adults seemed to talk of nothing else, but up to then there had been no bombing or anything to give me a clue as to what it was all about. Our only sources of news were the radio, or wireless as we called it, the newspaper or the cinema. The television was in its infancy and only had 25,000 viewers; we were not one of them. Actually, television was first broadcast from Alexandra Palace in August 1936. Its range was limited and only London and the eastern counties could receive it. We beat the Americans to television by five years and it was not until 1941 that they first broadcast. Screens were black and white of course. Everything went out live, there were no retakes like today, and if there were any mistakes they were there for all to see. The television showed such things as plays and sports, for example, the Boat Race, boxing matches and the FA Cup. Then at midday on 1 September 1939, they stopped broadcasting until 1946. Apparently it was believed that the short wave frequencies could guide enemy aircraft to their targets. The other factor was that many of their technicians joined up or transferred to radio, which was thought to be the better service. We are lucky today with twenty-four hours of coverage; in those days it was restricted. In our house we did not even have electricity; our lighting was by gas with mantles, which, if touched after being used, would shatter into hundreds of pieces. Of course, as a child I was curious and could not help climbing up and seeing them disintegrate.

In view of the fact that we had no electricity, our radio was run by an accumulator which we had to get charged at our local garage. The batteries were so heavy that Mum had to run them down to the garage on the pram. The process took a couple of days so Dad bought a spare battery so we had one charged all the time. There were 8½ million radio licences across the nation and although the sets looked primitive, being run on glass valves inside square boxes or the cat's whisker, and the sound sometimes faded, they were our main source of entertainment.

All this talk of war puzzled me and so one day I asked, 'Mum, what is war?' She looked at me, not quite knowing how to answer the question, and after a few moments replied, 'It's like you and your brother. When he wants something and you will not give it to him, what do you do? Fight! Countries are like that. Old Hitler wants more power and space and so he's fighting us for it.' I still did not quite understand.

Before war was declared in 1939, there was a sense of fear and trepidation in the adults. We children were excited and played soldiers with sticks as guns. Little did I know that some of our soldiers were so short of rifles that they were drilling with broomsticks! My father had joined the Territorials long before there was any talk of war and soon I noticed that he started going out for training more and more. He was out most nights and when he was made up to a sergeant, I remember Mum sitting in front of the fire in the front room sewing on his stripes. During the day he worked as a porter at Euston station and in later years he became a union leader. Although we were proud of him, he was like most fathers in those days – very strict! If I cheeked Mum or could not tie my shoelaces, he would pull my trousers down and bend me across his knee and whack me with his slipper until I bawled my eyes out. In those days it was an accepted way of keeping discipline and the saying was 'children should be seen but not heard'.

In September 1939, somehow everybody knew that Chamberlain was going to make a statement on the radio; it was on everyone's lips and grown-ups talked of nothing else. He had been to Munich in the previous September and came back waving a piece of paper on the steps of a plane. He declared 'peace for our time' but had surrendered part of Czechoslovakia. Hitler was not satisfied with this and stormed into Poland on 1 September 1939.

There was a sense of excitement and fear as we sat round the radio in the front room, Dad and me on one side and Billy sitting on Mum's lap on the other, each leaning forward to catch every word. I knew by the worried look on Mum's face that it was important. Suddenly, in solemn tones, the announcer said, 'the Prime Minister.' After that, I only remember the words 'and therefore we are at war with Germany' because the radio faded. For a moment, we just sat there, stunned. Within moments there was a loud wailing and Dad shouted, 'That's the air-raid warning. Get downstairs, in the basement. We'll get under that old table.' We rushed downstairs, Billy bouncing around in Mum's arms, while Dad urged me on. There was not enough room for Dad under the table and so he lay beside us, on an old sheet on the floor with his hands over his head. I don't know how long we stayed there but, to a young, energetic boy, it seemed a lifetime. I listened hard, expecting any moment for a bomb to come through our ceiling and kill us all.

After what seemed hours, a loud, continuous wail filled the air and not knowing what it was, I snuggled into Mum for safety. Dad laughed as he rose from the floor and shook his head, 'That must have been a practice run. I'm going outside for a smoke.' Everybody smoked in those days; normally if you were working class it was Woodbines. Suddenly, he came rushing in calling, 'Lou, Lou, [that was Mum's name] come and look at this!' We all trooped out into the back garden and at first I did not see what he was going on about until he pointed to the sky. I looked up and there were these giant silver balloons swaying about on long ropes.

'What are they, Dad?' I asked. Taking a puff on his cigarette he looked down at me, for he was over 6ft tall, and said, 'They're part of the air defence. It'll stop planes flying low and machine gunning us because if they touch one, they will go up in flames.' I was fascinated but could not see how they were going to deter the might of the German Air Force.

Soon after that day, Dad started packing up his kitbag and he and Mum seemed to cling to one another. Mum had tears in her eyes as she watched Dad moving around the house gathering up his things. He had been called up. The government conscripted men between eighteen and forty-one. In 1941, the age was put up to fifty-one but it was never really implemented and as far as it is known, no men over forty-five were called up. As Dad was in the Territorials, he was one of the first to go. Later, I learned that the government had brought in other powers, such as being able to seize any property they wanted; in restaurants there was a choice of only one meal; kites were banned; road signs were removed to confuse any enemy spies, and the government gave any wife whose husband had joined up protection against eviction.

Dad never showed me any affection but I remember him standing at the door, kissing Mum goodbye, and then he put his arm round me, drawing me close so that the material of his uniform tickled my nose and I could smell the distinctive scent of khaki. He whispered, 'You're the man of the house now. Look after your mother for me and behave yourself.' He kissed Mum again and we stood at the door and watched him till he turned the corner at the end of the street. We were on our own and I had this great responsibility of looking after Mum.

The day after our first air raid, after Aunt Milly had gone home, Mum put Billy in the pram, which bounced along, while I held on to the handle and ran alongside. I noticed changes in our road; there were gaps in the row of terraced houses and rubble lay everywhere. Some of the houses had no slates and their finger-like rafters reached for the sky. I had no idea where Mum was taking us but there was a sense of urgency in her stride. 'Mum, where are we going?' I blurted out as I ran along beside her, my legs hurting. 'I've got to get you away,' she replied, 'it's too dangerous.'

We turned the corner and there in front stood this tall, ornate building which I think was the Town Hall. Like most important buildings, it had sandbags piled up to the first floor. Some authorities protected their buildings in various other ways, often by constructing some sort of fence and filling boxes with earth.

She parked the pram just inside the door and asked the porter where she should go to get us evacuated. The man looked down at her and smiled, 'You should have gone the first time, love. Mind you, a lot have come back. The room's on the first floor' and he pointed up the winding stairs. Mum carried Billy, while I trailed behind as we climbed the steep, black marble stairs. I was fascinated by the paintings of what must have been previous mayors and the wooden panels. Exhausted, I looked up at Mum waiting at the top of the stairs. 'Come on, Jim,' she encouraged.

We walked along the very long passage, our steps echoing on the marble floor. In the distance sat a lady at a desk. Mum spoke to her and she indicated for us to sit down. Mum spoke to me in a whisper, 'Jimmy, pull your socks up.' They were always hanging round my ankles and seemed to be a constant worry to Mum but not to me. Suddenly, I jumped as the sound of a buzzer went off. 'You can go in now,' the lady said and opened the door. As we went through the door I saw a man sitting at a desk in the distance. He seemed to be miles away and we walked towards him, trying not to make too much noise. As we got close I could not help noticing that he had a moustache. The only person I had seen with one was Hitler. The man indicated to Mum to take a chair and while they talked I looked round the room, fascinated by the size of it and the decorations, especially the ceiling. It had, what many years later I learned, was egg and dart. Suddenly, my mum nudged my shoulder, waking me from my daydreams. 'The man spoke to you. Where do you want to go, the country or the seaside?'

You were never told where, that was kept secret. I had never left London before except on a coach trip to Southend, where we went out on a boat, and based on that, I made the right choice and blurted out, 'The seaside.' I spoke for both Billy and me; well, he could not speak, so somebody had to reply for him!

So it was decided that we were going to the seaside, if we lived long enough, for each night the German bombers returned, laying waste London. Mum decided that while we were waiting for a letter to come notifying us when we were going, we would not be safe under the table down in the basement, so each night she would pack some sandwiches, cold tea in a bottle, a few blankets and would walk to the Bethnal Green tube station, where she thought we would be safe. At first the London Underground authorities would not allow people to go down into the tube but public pressure soon changed their minds. Little did any one realize that on 3 March 1943, 173 people would lose their lives in Bethnal Green tube station, including forty-one children. Apparently as the crowds started to troop down the tube, a bus pulled up and people started streaming off just as the ack-ack started firing. Some people thought it was a bomb while others were frightened of the shrapnel raining down on them from the shells. They panicked and rushed forward, tumbling down the stairs onto the men, women and children in front

Newquay harbour, far away from the bombing in London.

of them who were crushed underfoot or against the walls. There was an account later of a child being lifted over the heads of the crowd and thereby being saved. The tube did accommodate vast numbers of London's citizens and at Bethnal Green that night, there were over 1,000 people. The slaughter was never reported and from accounts I have read, the next morning all the bodies had been cleared away and those on the platforms only heard rumours of the tragedy. The only thing that remained was piles of shoes. It was felt that if it was reported it would be bad for morale. Luckily for us, we were far away in Cornwall when this happened.

The first time we stayed in the tube, I can remember that we descended Bethnal Green's stairs, Mum first carrying Billy and most of the things we needed, including our gas masks, but I helped, struggling along with the food and drink in a paper carrier bag. As we went down the air below came up to greet us, bringing with it the smells and babble of over 1,000 people. At the bottom we stepped over, and sometimes tripped over, bodies lying on the passage floors. People swore at us but it was mostly good humoured; however, I learned a few swear words and got a clip round the ear from Mum later when I used them. On the platform itself, people lay in rows covered in anything they could find, from coats to blankets and sheets, on the cold platform. Later in the war I believe there were bunk beds. Somehow we found an empty space between some very fat, jolly women, who gave us some sweets, and a soldier and a girl, and we settled down for the night.

As I lay there, I heard a noise like distant thunder which got nearer and nearer and louder and louder. There was a rush of stale air sweeping along the platform. I curled up in fear, putting my hands over my ears wondering what was happening. Suddenly, a train roared in and stopped. As if by magic, the doors swept open and a few people got out. As they walked down the narrow passage between the sleepers and the edge of the platform, they tripped over feet and legs and again I added some colourful new words to my vocabulary which I quickly learnt were not for Mum's ears. I don't know if it was my imagination but the trains seemed to run all night and I would just drop off to sleep when another train would roar in. Eventually, after a few nights, I got used to it. As morning approached, I became aware of people moving around silently as they started to pack up their beds and gather up their belongings.

Bleary-eyed early morning workers began to crowd onto the platform ready to start their long day's work; Hitler was not going to stop them from doing their bit for the war effort. We climbed the dark, steep staircase and up ahead we could see a glimpse of daylight. As we moved out of the station entrance the daylight was blinding. Half asleep, I trailed behind Mum hanging on to her coat and dragging my feet. Looking round, I could not help but notice how last night's air raid had eaten into some of the streets; some were blocked off and we could see the rescue workers digging in the rubble, trying to pull people from the ruins of their houses. Like a row of teeth, houses which had been there the night before in straight lines looked broken and neglected. Roofs were stripped of their tiles, exposing the rafters which were twisted and bent by the bombing and pointed their witches' fingers to the sky. The roads were strewn with bricks and rubble. At the end of our road they had built a brick shelter, but one day when we came back from the underground, it was just a pile of bricks and we learned later that six of our neighbours who had been sheltering in there that night were killed. Apart from the tube and the public shelters, you could stay in Anderson shelters, which government had begun to issue before the war, costing 7s 6d plus labour charges. It was free to anybody earning less than £250 per annum. The shelter was made of curved, corrugated iron and dug into the garden with a brick wall at the entrance. In 1941, because many people liked to stay in their houses, Herbert Morrison brought out the Morrison shelter, which was similar to our old table but was made of metal.

An ordinary gas mask.

Morrison shelter.

Each time bombers came over the siren would go off and everyone would fly down to the nearest shelter and halt valuable production for the war effort. Often, the raids were just a single aircraft or were not in a particular area and so time was lost. They had people, normally air-raid wardens, nicknamed Jim Crows, watching from high roofs, factories and police stations for raiders. The government came up with a scheme so that aircraft warnings were more local; the alert, the alarm and the all clear. Although it was complicated for my young mind, I understood that if the alert sounded it should not interfere with normal life within that area, but the raiders were not too far away. People who were not working could, if they wished, take shelter, especially if they had children. Only if the Jim Crows thought the raid was overhead did they give the warning, then everyone took shelter.

Each day I raced Billy, which was not difficult considering his age, down the passage to the letterbox as the postman dropped our mail through. In those days we had two or three deliveries a day. We could not wait for the letter to arrive telling us what date we were to go and where. Finally it came and excitedly Mum opened it; we were going and because of Billy's age, Mum was coming with us. Down the tube station that night I could hardly sleep with thoughts of sea, sand and safety. We were advised not to take much and for us children, Mum limited us to just one favourite toy. I packed my lead soldiers into our case and Billy chose his teddy bear. Mum put them in our cases, out of the way, because children were not supposed to take toys.

Finally, the day came and there was no need for Mum to wake me as we put our last things into a tatty, brown suitcase and I held Mum's hand as I saw tears in her eyes as she took one last look round our home. Everything was supposed to be going into storage, supervised by Aunt Milly, but a fortnight after we arrived in Newquay we had a letter from her saying that a bomb had dropped on our house and everything had been destroyed, including my lead soldiers; regrettably I had changed my mind at the last moment and took a tin boat with me that I could sail on the sea.

———⚉———

Peter Butt was on holiday with his parents in Jersey when his father, who was a police officer in Bow, received a telegram ordering him to report back to his station as war was imminent. When they got home, Peter's mother was determined that Hitler was not going to spoil their break and so, leaving her husband behind, she went up to Yorkshire to visit Peter's grandmother,

Mrs Kettlewell, and his aunt and uncle, Elizabeth and Alan. At eleven o'clock on 3 September, they all gathered around the radio and froze when they heard Chamberlain declare Britain was at war. Immediately, his mother packed up their clothes and returned home with a view to getting her boys evacuated with their school, St Martin in the Fields, only to find the school had already been evacuated. His parents were worried and wondered what to do and so they made enquires about evacuation and within days, Peter, aged five, and his brother, aged ten, were standing at Paddington station heading for an unknown destination. After a journey which seemed to last for hours, they finished up in Highbridge, Somerset. Their foster parents' house was filthy and the woman fed them on jam sandwiches. When their mother came down to visit and saw how they were living, she took them home.

It was not long before the pair were on their way to Cambridge. They each took a vest, a pair of shorts, two pairs of socks, a pullover, handkerchiefs, shoes, and toiletries. They also took sufficient food for the journey. When they arrived at Cambridge station, they were given a paper bag of rations which was supposed to last forty-eight hours. It consisted of one tin of meat, two tins of milk, two packets of biscuits and a large bar of chocolate. The latter did not

Peter Butt's father (second from the left) and friends.

last long. They were well looked after by a vicar and his wife, but because of the Phoney War their mother took them back to London.. However, in June 1940, all hell broke loose as the Blitz started. At first they slept in the basement of the LEP Transport Offices but as the raids got heavier they slept in the underground at Covent Garden station. One morning when they emerged after a night of heavy bombing, they found their street blocked off. There were unexploded bombs and, for the third time, their mum arranged for their evacuation, this time to Redruth, Cornwall.

Like Peter and his brother, Harry Drury and his brother Roger were evacuated to Bedford in 1939 as soon as war was declared, but nothing had happened; there was no bombing. Their parents were missing them and could see no point in being separated and so, after two months, they brought them home.

Some time later, as they all slept in the family home, a bomb dropped about 400yds away and shook their world. It was enough to spur his parents on to have their two sons and their daughter, Eileen, evacuated. Dozens of children met up outside the public house called The Favourite at 8 a.m. not knowing where they were going. Suddenly, a number of coaches pulled up and they poured on in a babble of excitement. They travelled all day with frequent stops, as there were no toilets on board in those days. Finally, they reached Mylor Bridge, which is a small village near Falmouth. The coaches pulled up and they all streamed off into the little village school where they were greeted by Frances Smith, a lady in a Red Cross uniform. The villagers then started to select the child they wanted and slowly the hall started to empty until there were only five left. Harry, his brother, sister and the two Howard boys remained, but no villagers. Harry wondered what would they do and so he asked the question which worried him: 'What is going to happen to us?' Frances Smith replied, 'You are coming with me.' Little did they know what they were in for!

Mrs Patricia Free (née Wood) was one of the evacuees whose parents thought it best for her to leave in September 1939, straight after Poland had been invaded and they had heard the announcement 'Evacuate forthwith!' Early in the morning on 1 September she trooped down to her school, St James', carrying a bag of clothes, which included clean knickers. Bouncing on her shoulder was, of course, her gas mask. In accordance with instructions, she carried enough food for the day, but no drink. On the way she met up with her friend Moira Wise.

The children milling around, feeling lost.

At the school, they were all milling around until a teacher gave her a label to put on and ordered everyone onto the buses. At Paddington station her parents were not allowed on the platform to see her off. She had no idea where she was going, but it was a great adventure. After a long and gruelling journey, the school finished up in Madron, near Penzance, and tired and weary they were ushered on to the green of the village hall. People milled around choosing the child they wanted. Although exhausted, she was enthralled at being by the sea and was surprised and delighted when she and her friend were chosen by the same family. It must have been that, because they waited together, they were taken as sisters. The family that chose them already had an older daughter and a baby. They really treated the friends well.

Some children, like John Glyn, were evacuated privately. As soon as war was declared his parents sent him to Budleigh Salterton in Devon, and from there he went to Gloucester for a few weeks. However, there was very little bombing so like a lot of children, he went home to London. Later, when the bombing started in earnest, his parents decided he should be evacuated with the other children from White Hart Lane School in Wood Green to Cornwall.

Many organisations were involved with the evacuation, including schools, churches, synagogues and the police. Clive Mathison's father was a Metropolitan Police officer serving in North London. The family belonged to the Metropolitan Police Families' Association, who organised the family's evacuation to Falmouth while his father remained behind. His mother, twin brother and elder sister were billeted on a farm close to the River Fal. There was another family billeted with them but unfortunately they fell out with the farmer, and Clive's father had to arrange for them to return home, where the family suffered the horror of the Blitz.

Jean Pickering (née Desforges) was on holiday in Margate with her family when she became aware of her parents' concern about the situation in Europe and they were so worried they considered going home, but in the end the family finished off their holiday. It was a glorious summer and she can remember watching some Czech refugees swimming in the sea. They had come here after the Germans had occupied their country. Within two weeks of returning home, Jean and her sister Pat were evacuated, first of all to Brentwood, twelve miles outside London. Her mother had covered her gas mask case in Rexine and, to make her things easier to carry, had also given her a backpack. In Brentwood, she and the other evacuees were hawked round the town by the billeting officer, trying to find someone to take them in. Finally, a woman in Railway Terrace took them because 'that one looks like my dead sister.' The woman had four children of her own and she just loved young ones. Unfortunately, the baby had Down's syndrome. Jean's mother was always supplying extra food, bearing in mind it was rationed, including some homemade jam. The family were very poor and Jean can only remember having HP sauce on her bread, but never her mother's jam.

One day, a great row blew up over the fact that the eldest girl, aged sixteen, was going out with a married man; in those days that type of behaviour was frowned on. During the time of the Phoney War, because Brentwood was so near, Jean and Pat used to go home at weekends. Somehow, Jean let it slip about the sixteen-year-old daughter seeing a married man. Immediately, their mother brought them home but within a few months they were on a train with the other evacuees to Helston, Cornwall. The two sisters were billeted with the local doctor and Jean thinks the reason why he picked them was because of their French name, Desforges.

Frances Bishop was evacuated from Kings Cross, London, to Redruth in Cornwall when she was ten. Her father used to sit her down with her two sisters, Joan, aged eight, and Pat, who was only five, and explain what was going on in the world, including such things as the abdication, the Spanish War and the reasons for the war. He was very concerned about his wife, who was only 5ft tall, and he feared she would not be able to cope with the children when he got called up and the bombing started.

Like many, the girls were not evacuated in September 1939 but their parents waited until June 1940, when the Blitz started in earnest.

Living near the docks in London, with ships arriving every day with war material and food, it was imperative that Stan Mason was evacuated to somewhere safe. His parents decided not to part with him until it was absolutely necessary. When the bombing started in June 1940 they decided that it was time for their five-year-old boy to be evacuated under the government scheme. On the long journey to Cornwall, having never travelled before, Stan was fascinated by the rolling countryside and the animals.

At first, Eileen Penwarden's parents, who lived in Manor Park, London, decided that they would not evacuate her and her brother, David, but soon changed their minds when bombs started raining down out of the night sky. Eileen was ten when she and her brother, aged six, and their cousin started their journey at 7 a.m. from Cromwell School. Children from different schools in the area milled about in the playground as if they were lost while their teachers tried to get them organised. Eileen had no idea where she was going; it could have been the moon for all she knew. Parents started to cry, which set the children off. Finally, the teachers had them all settled in the coaches and with lots of waving and tears, they set off for Paddington station.

When she got there she could not believe the number of children on the platform waiting for the teachers and helpers to usher them onto the waiting train. The station was alive with children. Those parents who had followed the children to the station were kept outside and waited patiently in the hope of catching a glimpse of their child. To ensure everyone was there was worse than a recount at a local by-election, with recount after recount. Finally they were satisfied the numbers tallied. The train moved and as it did so she gripped her brother's hand, remembering her promise to her mother that she would look after him. She recalls wondering where they were going and, worst of all, whether she would ever see her parents again. Eileen's only experience of trains was when she visited her grandparents at Kelvedon. As far as she knew, this was a train to nowhere. The train stopped at several stations on the long journey where they were given drinks and sandwiches. She had no idea where she was as all the stations' names had been removed. When she thought the journey would never end the train pulled into a station and she heard the porter call out 'St Austell'. Tired and weary, she helped her brother off the train, making sure he had his case and gas mask with him.

There were many tears but big sister was there to wipe them away.

Outside the station they were herded onto waiting coaches and off they went again. They still did not know where they were going and it was several days before she learned that she was in Mevagissey. Some children were so tired they fell asleep on the way.

The coaches pulled up outside Chapel Hall. Frightened she was going to lose her brother, she kept hold of his hand. He was quite bewildered and lost. Inside the hall tables were laid out with cakes and children's treats. People were milling around, picking out the children who appealed to them. One woman pointed to her cousin and then her brother. Eileen's heart sank, but she held her brother's hand tightly, thinking, 'He doesn't go anywhere without me. He's my brother.' For a moment, Eileen thought the woman was not going to take the three of them but, after a pause, she nodded her head and took them. Eileen was pleased; she had kept her promise to her mother.

Professor Ken MacKinnon was on holiday at Boscombe with his parents when war was declared, but they were determined not to let the impending conflict spoil their first holiday since the depression. He was surprised to find that when he returned to London, it was as if the Pied Piper had spirited the children away. Like many families at that time, when the Blitz started they moved out to stay with relatives in the suburbs thinking they would be safer. Then they moved to Summer Court, a holiday home of one of his mother's friends, until one night in 1941 a bomb landed just behind the house, which was enough to convince them they were not far enough away from London and so they moved to St Ives in Cornwall. He was surprised to find that there were already many Londoners there from Millbank. Later in the war, when the Luftwaffe bombed Plymouth and tried to destroy the docks, many evacuees fled to St Ives from there, swelling the numbers.

When war was imminent, Ian Blackwell's parents arranged for him and his sister, Heather, to stay with a farmer in Shropshire. The old farm had no electricity or mains water. While he sat in the front room on 3 September, he froze as he heard Chamberlain's speech on an old radio which was run by accumulators. They were only at the farmhouse for three weeks when, because of the Phoney War, their parents took them back to London. They then booked him and his sister on the ill-fated SS *City of Benares* to Canada, under a scheme introduced in Wembley. They were both so excited that they could not contain themselves, when their parents suddenly cancelled it; they must have had a premonition, because the boat was torpedoed in the mid-Atlantic and sank. Most of the ninety children and crew were drowned, including Ian's friend Derek Goodfellow and his brother, Robin. One of the survivors went to Ian's school in London and everyone thought he was a hero.

In June 1940 the Blitz started and Ian's father built a brick shelter in the garden where, during the raids, they slept on bunk beds. His father also installed electricity. Each night Ian would lie in bed reading *The 39 Steps* and *King Solomon's Mines* while waiting for the bombing to start. At that time, shrapnel was a prized possession for most boys and on the way to school he would search for it; he was pleased one day when he found two pieces that fitted together.

Lying in the shelter one night, Ian heard the wail of a bomb and froze. He knew it would fall nearby. Suddenly, his world rocked as the sides of the shelter shook and he heard the blast of the bomb. When his family emerged from the shelter the next morning, they could not believe their eyes. Their windows had been blown out. It was obvious a bomb had dropped close-by. When they ventured inside the house, they found all the ceilings down and the place completely wrecked. His parents did no more but loaded up their car and set off to Gorran Haven in Cornwall.

Elsie and Rose from Bristol remember meeting up with other evacuees at Temple Meads station in 1939. Everyone was carrying their few belongings in small cases or bags. Around each child's neck hung their gas mask, and attached to them was a name tag.

The teachers who were going as well gathered them together. The air was heavy with excitement and anxiety as nobody knew where they were going. Being nine and eleven, the girls had different feelings. The younger sister thought it was great fun whereas the elder one worried about it, especially as they pulled away from the station and waved goodbye to their parents, not knowing when they would see them again.

The train sped through the open countryside and the journey went on and on. The sisters thought their journey was never going to end as station after station whizzed by. Just when they began to think it was going to go on forever, the train started to slow down and pulled into Truro. They had arrived!

Some children were evacuated twice or even three times. As the war progressed, certain places that were thought to be safe became the opposite, especially when the doodlebugs and V2s started to rain down from across the English Channel. Anne Vaughan, who was seven, and her sister, Jill, were initially evacuated with their school, St Vincent's Convent. Most of the pupils and teachers were billeted in Leigh, Essex, but she and a few others went on to Fordcombe, where she was billeted with a Mr and Mrs Mitchell. Then, after a year, they were moved to The Causeway, Kent. She remained there through most of the war until the doodlebugs started to fly across the channel and occasionally fall short of their London target, so she was moved to a country mansion in Trewithian, Cornwall, which was the home of Squire and Mrs Johnson; she could not believe her luck!

It took the outbreak of war for Marjorie Pascoe to return to the place where her father had been born, Penryn in Cornwall. Unfortunately, he had been killed in an engineering accident when she was only three. In August 1939 she had just returned from holiday, near Great Yarmouth, when she was told to go to her school in West Ham to be fitted out with a gas mask; as they put it over her face she found she could not stand the smell and, thrusting her fingers under the rubber, threw it as far away as she could.

A little later she noticed that her mother was packing and thought they were going on holiday again. Next morning a London taxi arrived outside the door to take her, her father's sister, her cousin Derek, her aunt's sister-in law and her young baby down to Cornwall. Marjorie and her cousin sat cramped on the two tip-up seats. The driver stayed with them that night and next morning was given a Cornish pasty for the journey back to London. They stayed there for a year and because it seemed that only the ports were being bombed, the family returned to London – but soon the Blitz got into full swing.

An air-raid warden holding up an incendiary bomb.

The family attended the wedding of Marjorie's youngest uncle. They had just sat down to the meal when the air-raid warning went off. Quickly, they abandoned the food and were ushered into the wire-meshed cloakroom. She sat on one of her uncle's knees while her cousin, Derek, sat on the other. The raid raged outside while they sat there waiting patiently for the all clear. When it came, people started drifting home. Marjorie and her family caught a bus. Halfway home an air-raid warden stepped out and, raising his hand, stopped the bus and told them to get off. In the street ahead they could see flames leaping up from houses which had been set alight by incendiary bombs. The ARP men guided them away from the scene through roads and alleys. Suddenly, Marjorie looked up and to her surprise saw an airman floating down towards a barrage balloon. She tried to stop and watch but her mother pulled her away. She never did find out what happened to the airman. As soon as they got home the siren went again and they spent the night in the Anderson shelter. After that her mother decided she had had enough and it was time to return to Cornwall, but this time they went by train.

2

THE JOURNEY

Evacuees streamed out of the ten designated evacuation areas of London, Chatham, Portsmouth, Birmingham, Liverpool, Manchester, Sheffield, Newcastle and the Scottish cities of Edinburgh and Glasgow to reception areas all over the country.

3,000 buses and 4,000 trains were used to convey this army of 1½ million evacuees to their destinations. Between 28,000 and 34,350 children were evacuated to Cornwall. To give some idea of the numbers, when train no. 116 steamed out of London it had 230 mothers and children who were bound for Cornwall. Stations put up notices stating that normal services would be interrupted and that the evacuees' trains had priority. It was subsequently found that the government had overestimated the numbers of children going and some vehicles were not needed due to parents who had changed their minds at the last moment and found that they could not bear the thought of parting with their children.

Some trains had no corridors and so children were confined to their carriages for hours on end, unable to use the toilet. Roads were made one way so that the coaches could get through. Some of the reception areas did not receive the evacuees they were expecting. One area was told they were going to have expectant mothers and made plans accordingly but actually received children, which was a headache for the billeting officer. Some trains arrived half-empty and foster parents went away disappointed, as in some villages in Yorkshire, but in other areas more arrived than had been planned for, which meant the billeting officer had to beg to get people to take the extra children. Despite some breakdowns of the plans, on the whole the evacuation went well, considering the vast number of people involved.

As my mother closed the front door behind us in September 1940, Mrs Wilson from next door came out and, with tears in her eyes, hugged her and gave my brother Billy and me a shilling, which was a fortune in those days, and all I could think about was how I was going to spend my half. As some of the other neighbours were on their knees, whitening their front steps, they stood and waved, 'Good luck, Lou, have a good journey.' Mum had told most people we were going as she did her shopping down Bethnal Green Road. The roads seemed to be alive with children running along beside their mothers. Groups of children gathered in the school playgrounds while their tearful mothers hugged them and said their goodbyes. For many, although they did not know it, it would be the last time they would see their parents as the German air raids took their toll. All the children had two things in common; hanging around their necks was a little brown box, containing their gas mask, and each wore a name tag either on their lapel or their arm. There were four types of gas masks; the normal one, which I had and hated because I could hardly breathe; a Mickey Mouse one with red ears which Billy had; one for young babies, which was a bit like an iron lung, and I learned later there was one for people who had to deal with gas bombs which had great goggle eyes which frightened the life out of me.

The night before we went, we did not go down the tube as Mum wanted to get up early the next morning, so we slept under the table in the basement on an old mattress. When we arrived at Bethnal Green tube station people were still asleep and so we made our way carefully along the platform, trying not to trip over their feet and fall onto the lines. Mum had warned us to be careful, as the lines were electric and if we touched them, they would kill us. That was beside what Mum would do! On the tube train, I can remember people smiling at us as Billy and I sat still for the first time in our lives as we watched the passengers come and go. We were dressed in our best clothes, as Mum said it saved packing them and said she would kill us if we mucked them up. I remember seeing a soldier with his kitbag resting on the floor, but what fascinated me was his rifle, which he had slung over his shoulder. I had never seen one before and longed to touch it.

At Paddington station we got on the escalator, which terrified me. Mum said, 'Whatever you do, don't get caught under the teeth of the stairs.' Mum stepped on with Billy balanced on one arm and our case in the other. I followed behind, like the chuck wagon, with our sandwiches and cold tea in a brown carrier bag. I wavered at the top of the stairs, watching Mum and Billy disappear into the distance.

Finally I summoned up the courage to leap on over the teeth. Our food bag bounced against the rail. Lucky the bottle of tea did not smash. I descended into the depths and felt the air coming up to greet me. There at the bottom I could see the teeth waiting for me as the stairs disappeared under them and they got nearer and nearer. I could imagine myself being dragged underneath, never to be seen again. At the last moment I leaped off and fell against a well-upholstered woman, again saving the tea, although she was not very pleased. I didn't mind because I had escaped the teeth!

As we entered Paddington station I could hear great trains steaming and puffing away like dragons breathing fire. Everywhere there seemed to be children milling about in groups. Some, like me, had their mothers with them; others were supervised by volunteers who had armbands on with the letters LCC, standing for London County Council. Apparently, parents who were not travelling with their children were not allowed in the station and had said their goodbyes in the playgrounds of hundreds of schools throughout London. The same was happening in all the evacuation areas throughout the country. There was a buzz of excitement in the air as hundreds of children talked at the same time. Mum grabbed my hand and said, 'I don't want to lose you here, I'll never find you and you might finish up in Timbuktu!' I wondered where that was.

An announcement came over the tannoy and Mum pulled me through the gates to join a queue where a woman with a clipboard ticked off our names. Everybody seemed to be helping in this chaotic world. I saw a large policeman carrying a baby on each arm for a mother who was struggling with her case. Porters held the hands of little children and guided their mothers to their seats and settled them in. It was as if everyone was going on a holiday. The noise of hundreds of excited children and trains getting up steam for their journeys to different parts of the country engulfed the station. Mum hustled us into a carriage, putting our old battered case on the rack and, with a sigh of relief, sat down.

Outside children scurried about trying to find a suitable carriage. A tubby lady staggered in with her son, Tony, who was about my age and his sister, Alice, who was a little older. Tony and I formed an instant bond as we looked across at one another. Their mother, Mrs Parsons, started talking to Mum and in no time it looked like they had been friends for years as they shared their experiences. Suddenly the door was opened by a porter and a smartly dressed lady came in with her two boys in blazers. I looked across at Tony and grinned. We knew they were not our type and hated them from the start. Mrs Snooty, as she became known to all, opened her purse and took out some money and handed it to the porter. I saw Mum smirk at Mrs Parsons. Mrs Snooty's boys sat opposite me and

Clive, the eldest of the two, poked out his tongue. I did it back. My mum missed very little, including my ear!

We waited there while the latecomers arrived as the train puffed gently like a sleeping giant, suddenly awakening when the porter blew his whistle to signal we were off on a journey of a lifetime!

———⟨⟨⟨———

When John Glyn arrived at Paddington station with his school, he was carrying his small suitcase, his label with his details and, of course, his gas mask. He had no idea where he was going. He sat on the train looking out for his parents, who had not been allowed on the platform. Suddenly, he saw them two tracks away waving madly. He thought his heart would break. Opposite him a small girl was grasping a penny which her mother had given her as a keep-sake. She sat there clutching it all the way to Newquay, possibly wondering if she would ever see her mother again, as if the penny was their only remaining link. When she finally opened her hand many hours later, John swears her palm was green from the bronze.

Not everybody went down to Cornwall by train. One bright sunny Sunday, Professor Ken MacKinnon was driven, in a hired car, all the way to St Ives by a Mr Stribley. They travelled via the scenic route and he can remember beauty spots like Hells Mouth, but nothing compared to his first sight of St Ives, which left an indelible impression on him. He had seen it on posters at railway stations and had never thought he would see it in real life, but there it was spread out before him and all because of the war.

The car had threaded its way through the narrow streets of St Ives searching for Academy Cottage, which had been recommended by some East End friends. His Aunt Pat and Uncle Harry had lodgings with the Coach family next door and he was taken in by two elderly spinsters. Soon he was introduced to the other guests at the property, who were merchant seamen. St Ives was a port where convoys mustered, and therefore the sailors came and went frequently. They were of all different nationalities: Belgians, Canadians and Welsh, who, when they sat down to meals, would teach him a few words of their language. His favourite guest was a Canadian from Vancouver. He was short and stocky and always wore a white, roll-necked sweater and would sit crossed-legged on a rocker in the kitchen to knit white string vests with big, wooden needles. Everybody had a go at knitting during the war.

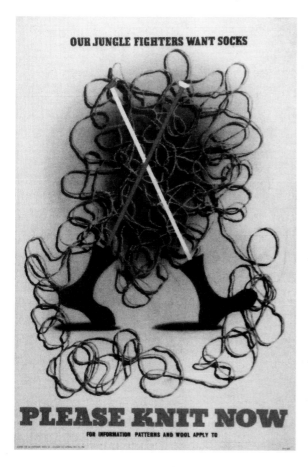

Everybody knitted.

One morning, Ken came down for breakfast and found Miss Perkins crying. She was holding a telegram and Ken knew by the look on her face that it was bad news. His Canadian friend had gone down with his ship after it had been torpedoed. That incident brought home the stark realisation that the true cost of imported food was, in fact, sailors' lives.

Two other evacuees who did not travel to Cornwall by train were Ian Blackwell and his sister, Heather. Their father set off by car to Cornwall, on what was in those days a hazardous journey. What did not help was that all the road signs had been taken down to confuse the enemy. Everything went well until they reached Exeter, where they got lost and drove across Dartmoor. Although their father had gone the wrong way, Ian and his sister were thrilled when they saw Dartmoor Prison looming out of the mist. The car chugged along at an average speed of 30mph, which was considered good in those days.

Finally, after many hours, they found the place they were looking for – Gorran Haven on the south coast of Cornwall. But they still had to find Mr and Mrs Seville's bungalow. They went round and round and at last they found the place. Finally, tired and weary, Ian and his sister washed and crawled into bed, their minds full of the things that they had experienced on the long journey from London. They couldn't help but wonder what adventures awaited them in Cornwall.

Mrs Frances Bishop travelled by train from Paddington and recalls that it was a glorious day when she and her two sisters left home early to make their way to Lion Street School in Islington, which was not her normal school. Their father thought it would be easier for them to have backpacks rather than suitcases. When they arrived at the school there seemed to be hundreds of children, parents and officials hanging about, not knowing what was happening. Suddenly a fleet of charabancs pulled up outside and the children were ushered on to the buses. Each child was issued with a lunch box. The only thing she can remember that was in it was a Buzz, which was a chocolate biscuit in a yellow wrapper with a bee on it.

After everybody was accounted for, the coaches roared into life and the girls only just had enough time to wave to their parents before they were off. They were not told where they were going or what railway station they were leaving from. Being enterprising, Frances' father found out and organized a taxi to take her mother and a few neighbours to Paddington station, but when they got there they were not allowed in, and so Frances and her sisters never saw them. To a young girl, Paddington station seemed enormous, dirty and noisy. There was total pandemonium. The coaches drove directly onto the platforms and the gates were locked, barring the parents. She heard mothers pleading and crying to be let through to see their children off but the authorities were adamant; no parents were allowed in.

There seemed to be thousands of children and the officials kept dashing up and down the platform, counting the children again and again. One of the helpers looked very curious; he was tall and skinny and dressed in a Scout's uniform, with a tall, pointed hat. Suddenly he grabbed Frances by the scruff of the neck yelling, 'Here he is!' She was puzzled, she had never been called a 'he' before, but apparently they had one more boy's name on the list than there should have been and one extra girl. Somebody had spelled Frances the boy's way. She thought it was her fault and that she was holding up the war effort.

While they had been trying to find the missing boy their train was holding up a train coming into the station. Its blinds were pulled down and you could not see inside. Finally, the dark train pulled onto the platform opposite. Frances stared in amazement as large groups of doctors, nurses and orderlies filled the platform. Suddenly, the carriage doors opened and out stumbled men in tattered uniforms who were pale as death, dirty, and exhausted. Some were even naked, with no boots, clutching a blanket round them. These were just the walking wounded who could hobble along by themselves. Soon, an army of doctors, stretcher bearers and orderlies began lifting off the badly wounded. It was obvious that the authorities did not want the children to see. Frances found out much later that what she had witnessed was some of the survivors of Dunkirk disembarking.

Fortunately the train that was going down to Cornwall was a long one, with a corridor. The journey went on and on for hours and the carriage became hot, stuffy and very noisy. Frances' little sister, Pat, was a bad traveller and this seemed to be a journey to the end of the world. She was sick and complained of a headache. Frances had promised her mother she would look after her; there was nobody else. She took her to the toilet and washed her face and hands, wetting her hanky to keep her cool. Pat was only five and it made a long journey seem longer.

At the age of four and a half, Michael Duhig and his eleven-year-old twin brothers, Paddy and Billy, were evacuated with St Mary and Joseph's School from Poplar to Truro. All he remembers about the journey from Paddington was being in a compartment with some of the teachers and kneeling on the floor, clutching two pennies. After the long journey the three of them walked to a nearby school where they were separated.

Michael was taken to a hostel where there were a number of other young children. They slept on camp beds, with the girls in another room. The children were put to bed and the lights were turned out at 6 p.m. sharp. The room was in complete darkness because of the blackout blinds. The disconcerting thing was that as he lay there, he could hear other children outside playing.

The lady who ran the hostel was called 'matron' and the other assistants were nurses. For breakfast every morning they had porridge and they were made to eat every scrap of food that was put in front of them.

Edna Goreing (née Lazzerini) was seven at the time of her evacuation. She remembers being squashed up in a corner by a fat teacher all the way from

London to Cornwall and having to go out into the corridor for fresh air. Like many of the evacuees, she found the journey long and tiring.

Munching cream crackers and cheese between sucking boiled sweets from her small knapsack, Mary Garnham, then aged seven, remembers sitting next to her sister on the long, hot journey, which she describes as a nightmare, from Senior Street Primary School, Paddington, to Penzance railway station. When they finally arrived they were taken to Sancreed Church School, about four miles outside Penzance. There, they were lucky enough to be selected by Miss Mabel Wherry, who was single and lived with her parents. They stayed with them all through the war and got to love them so much they used to call them Grandma and Granddad.

—◦◦◦—

I had never been on a steam train before and could feel the power as the wheels started to turn. A cheer went up from one end of the train to the other as every child, except two, yelled at the top of their voices. Clive and his brother, Edward, sat there, not showing any expressions other than 'What's all the fuss about, after all, it's only a train journey!' The train gathered speed and Tony and I opened the window and put our heads out, feeling the wind and smoke in our faces. Mum, as usual, was worried, saying, 'Don't put your heads out too far, you might get them knocked off!' but we took no notice, and all down the train could be seen children's heads poking out from each carriage. Suddenly, there was a whoosh and a train in the opposite direction came thundering by and we both fell back in hysterics. We thundered over bridges where below we saw trams snaking along their lines while horses and carts gently trotted along the roads. From our vantage point we could see where the nightly raids had damaged rows of terraced houses, leaving gaps of nothing but rubble, but life was going on as people below went about their daily business.

As we moved out into the suburbs, many houses were no longer set out in terraces and it was noticeable that there was not so much bomb damage. The houses had big gardens and there were no tin baths hanging on the back walls on nails, like at home. Suddenly, the constant rhythm of the rail changed as we sped out into the country. Most of us East End kids had never seen the countryside before and we watched in awe as we sped past sheep, cows and pigs. Tony shouted, 'Look, look, there's a rabbit!' One of the snooty kids huffed, as if the sight was commonplace and perhaps to them it was, but to us, every inch we travelled was something new. We were on the journey of a lifetime. As we passed over level crossings, children, and occasionally their parents, waved coloured scarves and white handkerchiefs over the gates, and our arms nearly dropped off in our enthusiasm to wave back. We flashed past stations whose names had been painted out to fool the enemy. It certainly fooled us!

Suddenly, Tony pointed to the sky and shouted, 'There are two planes heading for us.' Mum pushed me out of the way and looked out of the window. 'It's alright, they're ours.' They came back several times, and each time I wondered if Mum was right, but I assumed if they had been enemy planes they would have fired on us.

After they had gone and we had settled down, we soon became bored. We hadn't the room in our cases to bring any games and so we played 'I Spy' but Billy did not understand the idea, which was unsurprising considering his age. Mum suggested we sang and soon we were roaring out such tunes as 'Ten Green Bottles', 'Doing the Lambeth Walk' and 'Daisy, Daisy'. Mum and Mrs Parsons started singing 'Roll Me Over in the Clover' and kept smirking at one another while Mrs Snooty looked disapprovingly at them, and I could not understand why. Soon the sandwiches came out and Mum offered our fish paste ones round, but Mrs Snooty shook her head. Mrs Parsons took one and offered us her cheese sandwiches in return. Later, Mrs Snooty discreetly took her sandwiches out of a cane case but did not hand them round. They smelled fishy and I now suspect they were smoked salmon; too good for the likes of us! We drank cold tea out of a bottle while she poured hot steaming tea out of, what I now know, was a Thermos flask.

Soon the grown-ups were asleep and I can remember creeping out into the corridor and going mad. We ran up and down. Soon children from other parts of the train joined us. With difficulty we played 'He', but there was just no room to dodge. Suddenly, the guard threw open one of the connecting doors and stood there glaring, his hands on his hips. He asked angrily, 'What's all this then?' and we scattered like frightened rabbits back to our carriage, hoping he would not tell Mum. I did not want another of her famous clips round the ear.

We were all bored, hot and tired; even the Snooty boys had taken off their ties. The place we were going to was another world, but where was it? We had been travelling for hours. I was woken up by the change of the train rhythm and realized the train was pulling into a station. I put my head out and there on the platform were what seemed to be dozens of people standing about. Mrs Snooty said, 'It's Taunton' in her condescending voice. Doors were opening and some of the evacuees were being herded off by their supervisors. One girl forgot her gas mask and had to go running back while her supervisor waited impatiently with her hands on her hips. They were lined up like soldiers and, tired and weary, they marched off. The train whistle blew and we were off again.

The train was half-empty and we had great fun walking the length of it. We had started out early in the morning and it was now getting dark. There were no lights on the train as the authorities feared a light would be seen by the German aircraft. There was petrol rationing and so there were few cars on the road and they also had their lights shielded, with only a small cross shining out. Petrol was rationed by the size of the engine and in some cases four gallons had to last a month. Later on in the war petrol for private cars was stopped all together but, of course, there was always the black market, which was both dear and illegal.

I kept asking Mum that age-old question that children have asked throughout the years: 'Mum, when will we get there?' I don't think she knew any more than I, but she replied, 'In a moment, son, in a moment.'

It was now pitch black outside and we were drawing into another station. I was half asleep when I heard a voice say 'Newquay!' We had arrived. Somebody, I don't know who, helped me off the train and outside the station on to the steps

On their way, but nobody knew where.

of a single-decker bus and I flopped on the seat. The next thing I knew was that Mum was shaking me and the cold night air drifted in from the open bus door and wearily I stepped down. My breath was taken away as I saw, silhouetted in the moonlight, the Great Western Hotel, with the noise of the sea crashing into the caves below.

The evacuees had arrived! The hotel staff were used to more refined clients and did not know what was about to hit them!

⟨⟨⟨⟩⟩⟩

After the long journey from London, five-year-old Stan Mason was exhausted and staggered off the train with his few belongings. He was shepherded to a place called Constantine, a short distance from Falmouth. He recalls that at that time it only had one street, one pub, and a few shops way out in the countryside. He could not help comparing it with London, where everything was just round the corner, but in Constantine, it was all farmland, fields and cottages.

Tired and weary, all the evacuees stumbled up to the church at the top of the village, with frequent stops to catch their breath as they dragged their cases behind them. In the darkening church, they waited patiently to be selected by the crowd of local people before them. Stan looked around worriedly as child after child was selected. He was sure nobody wanted him but he was wrong. Mr and Mrs Laity stopped before him and pointed, 'We'll have him!' He found that they lived in a tiny cottage at the bottom of an extremely steep hill, in a place called Penjerrick, which had five other houses. The property had two bedrooms, a tiny lounge, and a scullery. It had no running water and he soon learned that the water was obtained from a pump 50yds away and it had to be fetched in a large jug. There was no electricity or gas and at night the paraffin lamps were lit. The worst thing of all was that the toilet was in the garden.

Towards the end of the war, Mrs Laity fell ill and could no longer care for him and so it was arranged that Mr and Mrs Pascoe, who lived near the bottom of Constantine, should take him in. Stan was delighted because the house had electricity and running water. On the first night he could not help turning the light on and off; unfortunately his game played havoc with the Pascoes' radio. They were a good family, but they were sticklers for mealtimes and he got into trouble on a number of occasions because, like most boys, he had no idea of time.

Sitting on the train at Paddington station on 18 June, Ellen Murt, who was eight, listened to the train gently puffing out steam before it pulled away on its journey into the unknown. Nobody knew they were going to Cornwall. The weeping parents were behind the barriers, having been barred from entering the station. Suddenly, Ellen heard the air-raid warning and she put her arms round her two younger sisters. Her mother had told her she must look after them and they must stick together. She sat there, wondering what was going to happen. Suddenly, all hell broke out. Some of the waiting parents panicked at the sound of the air-raid warning and forced their way into the station. They pushed the police and helpers aside and started dragging their children out of the carriages, while the police pushed the frightened, screaming children back. It was like a mad house. To everyone's relief, the all clear sounded. It was a false alarm and the mayhem quietened down, but many of the children on that train never made the journey to the safety of Cornwall but instead went back to the hazards of the daily raids and the Blitz while Ellen and her sisters started their great adventure.

After a long journey they finally arrived at Truro and disembarked. They were all ushered round the back of the cathedral and given something to eat and drink. They were then all packed onto coaches and taken to different parts of Cornwall, but all the time Ellen held on to her sister's hand with her arm around the other one. Wherever they were going, they were going together, but when they got to St Agnes they did get split up, despite her protests. Her young sister stayed with her while her other sister went across the road to a nice family.

Eileen Penwarden, her brother David and her cousin were taken from Chapel Hall in Truro to a house not far away after her terrible journey from London. Although it was ten o'clock at night and the sun was sinking, it was double summer time and they were asked if they wanted to go for a walk. The women took them down to the harbour and out on the quay. They had only seen the sea once or twice in the past, and they simply stood in awe. That night, she shared the daughter's bedroom but during the night she heard her brother crying in the next room. The day had been traumatic for them all. The next day she asked if she could sleep in his room and they agreed.

Their foster family treated them well and they were made part of the family. When the family visited their relations they took Eileen and her brother with them and they were always treated as one of the family. The family widened Eileen's culinary experiences by introducing her to pasties, under-roast and yeast and saffron cakes.

The train was in uproar when Ken Foxon boarded it at Paddington station. His parents decided not to evacuate him in 1939, but when the bombing started in June 1940 they decided it would be safer out of London and so, on 14 June, he was taken to Duncan Road School in Upper Holloway, where he waited in the playground. He had no idea where he was going or when he would see his parents again. His parents gave him a final hug before he boarded the bus for the journey into the unknown. All around, children cried as they stared out of the coach window at their parents standing below, waving goodbye, and then they were off to heaven knows where.

Ken relates that the train journey was long and boring after they got over the thrill of seeing the countryside and animals in the fields. For a while they played games of 'Snakes & Ladders', 'Ludo' and 'I Spy', then they ran up and down the corridor until they were told off. Finally, after it seemed their journey would never end, they reached St Ives, where, tired and weary, they were lined up and marched up to a school. Ken describes it like a cattle market as people came in to select the child they wanted. Mr and Mrs Delve wanted a little girl but finished up with Ken, who considered himself the luckiest boy on earth that they had chosen him. The family had three daughters and being the only boy in the household, the girls thoroughly spoilt him. It was ironic in as much as, years later, his son married Susan, a daughter of one of the girls.

When will we see you again?

3

WE SETTLE IN

The year before the war started, a survey of the reception areas had been carried out by local councils who, in some cases, had delegated the task to the parish councils because of a lack of staff. They visited every property in their area, be it a manor house or humble cottage, to ascertain what spare rooms were available. The residents were then told, not asked, how many evacuees they would have to take. If they objected or refused they could be fined or imprisoned, and a few were. The staff who carried out the survey did so on a voluntary basis and the councils had to be constantly reminded of the urgency of the situation in order to complete the task.

Foster parents were paid 10s 6d for the first child and 8s 6d for any additional child. For mothers with young children or expectant mothers, the landlord was paid 5s 6d plus 3s for each child. The landlord was paid 5s for housing a teacher or helper, but they had to feed themselves. Most evacuees were lucky because the people who looked after them cared, but there were exceptions. Some children finished up in manor houses while others lodged with farmers and farm workers. The greatest enemy of the evacuees was homesickness, and most suffered from it.

―――✼✼✼―――

Wearily I pushed open the glass door of the Great Western Hotel for my mother, who was struggling with my baby brother in one arm and a case in the other. It was midnight and we had been travelling all day, but the grandeur of the hotel took our breath away. Coming from the East End of London we just stood and stared, feeling out of place at the unaccustomed luxury. The floor was carpeted and in the entrance hall windows hung beautiful, velvet curtains – which were soon removed after we arrived! We were led into the dining room, the floor of which had been devotedly polished for years and was a credit to the hard work of the staff. You could see your face in it. Set out were bare tables in a long line with silver cutlery which, after that first meal, we never saw again. After that, everybody had to supply their own. The only thing we had eaten all day was the sandwiches and we were starving. The staff, who I am certain had never seen such a ravenous lot, gingerly placed before us plates of fishcakes, mashed potatoes and peas, which were instantly scoffed down. I have hated fishcakes ever since! We had pears and custard as afters, which the Snootys called 'sweet', a thing we never had at home. When we had wolfed down the food, the tables were put to one side, exposing the beautiful wooden floor. The grown-ups were taken into the bar for a talk on what was expected of them and to be allocated their rooms while we children, who had been cooped up all day, found new reserves of energy and went mad in the beautiful skating rink of a ballroom. It did not take us long to learn that the chairs, which had curved steel runners, could be used as sledges, and so years of hard work polishing the floor were destroyed within moments. We ran a few yards, pushing the chair in front of us, before leaping

The Great Western Hotel.

on and sliding the length of the room. In no time at all there were deep gouges in the wood. It was wonderful, until the manager appeared at the entrance, tearing his hair out. We ignored him; we were having so much fun until the voices of authority cut in, 'You little bastards! Pack it in or we'll beat the life out of you!' We stopped instantly; it was a language we understood. When we left three years later, the floor was still marked and was a dirty grey, trodden in over the years we were there by more than fifty pairs of feet.

Wearily, Mum washed us down in a bowl with cold water from a jug. I was worn out and climbed into the soft double bed, which I shared with Billy while Mum slept in a single bed at the bottom of ours. I pulled the covers over me and slept like I have never slept before or since. The fear of being killed had vanished and, although it would return, at that moment in time I felt safe.

Whereas we went to a hotel, when John Glyn got off the train he was taken to a school where, as was the practice, the process of selection began. Two elderly teachers, Mr and Mrs Martin, selected him and another boy called Clive Rogers. When they arrived home, all they wanted to do was sleep but they were bathed in scalding hot water. They both cried, which is not surprising when you think of the long journey they had just undertaken.

The Martins were good foster parents but found two healthy, boisterous boys too much for them, so they saw the billeting officer, who arranged for the Revd Price and his wife to foster them. They lived on Mount Wise and John and Clive spent the rest of their time in Cornwall with them. Although they were not like his parents, they made good substitutes. Some winter nights, with the fire roaring in the background, they all stood round the piano singing popular songs of the time at the top of their voices, such as Vera Lynn's 'White Cliffs of Dover' and Diana Durbin's 'Waltzing in the Air'.

On that first morning in Newquay, I remember waking with the sun streaming through the window, the dust dancing and sparkling in its beam. Mum was still snoring for England in the other bed and so, slipping out, I crept across to the window and stood in awe. The sea was roaring in, hurling itself against the cliffs below. In the distance I could see the fragile bridge which led across to an island.

To me as a child, it looked a magical castle which was guarded by a dragon who had imprisoned a beautiful princess within its walls. I had to visit this far-off land and so I threw on my clothes, which I had dropped on the floor the night before, and now found that some fairy had kindly put them on the back of a chair. Without washing, I crept out into the passage, gently closing the door behind me. There was nobody about and so I slipped downstairs and out of the door. Outside, the sea breeze blew directly into my face, which made it tingle. For a moment I stood in the courtyard taking in the view and trying to find my bearings. In the distance, I could see some houses; they looked all intact, there was neither a slate missing nor a window broken. It looked to me that the war had not reached this part of Cornwall.

I followed the road down and at the bottom could see the harbour, with its small ships fighting with their anchors. As I walked, an old man came struggling up the hill with a box on his shoulders. He was about to pass me when he paused and, looking straight at me, said something I could not understand. I must have looked an idiot to him as I stood there, trying to make out what he was saying. Finally, I realized he was asking if I was one of them there evacuees. 'Yes, I am.'

'You'll be safe enough here, boy. Come from London, do 'ee?' I nodded. I could just make out that he thought we were having a rough time in London and again I nodded.

'What you got in the box?' I asked, having a good idea by now as the smell had reached me. He lifted the box down from his shoulder and held it out. It was full of fish. 'It's taken me all night to catch these. I'm taking them up to the hotel. See you, boy!' He grunted something else and was on his way.

I began to worry and thought I'd better get back. As I entered the hall, Mum was there in an agitated state talking to one of the women. My heart sank. I knew I was in for it and I was not mistaken as I received another of Mum's famous clips round the ear.

—◦∕◦∕◦—

When Frances Bishop and her sisters, Joan and Pat, finally arrived in Redruth, Cornwall, it might have been Timbuktu for all she knew. She had no idea where Cornwall was, except it was a very long way from home. It took the evacuees what seemed like hours to disembark because the children were tired, weary and hungry. Despite how Frances felt, she could not help standing and admiring the setting sun disappearing over the horizon. Outside the station they were ushered on to a bus and set off into the night.

They finally pulled up outside Barncoose School in Chariot Road, where, wearily, they all filed into a hall and flopped on the floor. Frances was so tired, lost and bewildered that night that she does not remember having anything to eat or drink, all she wanted to do was sleep. For what seemed an eternity the evacuees sat or lay on the floor exhausted, almost oblivious to groups of people appearing, selecting a child or two and leaving. It was like a dream. Gradually, the hall emptied and the three sisters still sat there, sad and forlorn, waiting to be picked. Joan and Pat stretched on the floor, closed their eyes and slept. When they woke up, the hall was almost empty. All the children had gone; it appeared nobody wanted them. Several grown-ups stood in a group, their heads bowed, deep in conversation. They kept looking in the girls' direction. It was obvious they did not know what to do with the three sisters. Finally, they were crammed into the back of a small black car and sped off into the night. A man was driving while a woman sat beside him looking down at her clipboard. Suddenly, the car jerked to a halt in Barncoose Terrace. The man grunted as he slipped from the car and started knocking on each door down the street. It was now pitch black but Frances could see people shaking their heads. Nobody wanted them! In the back of the car the two younger sisters started to cry, which did not help.

In one last, desperate effort, the billeting officer ordered the girls out of the car and wearily knocked at No. 15 with the three girls standing beside him. The door opened and a young, dark woman opened it. She listened, with her head on one side, and then spoke over her shoulder to a tall, dark young man. A small boy in pyjamas pushed his head between the two of them. The couple kept looking at the three girls and then one another. It was obvious they were in two minds. Then, with a shrug of her shoulders and a nod from the man, she beckoned the three of them in. Somebody wanted them. Wearily, they stumbled up the steps. The young couple, Jean and Donald Wills, washed the girls and then sat them down to a meal. They were joined by their young son, Gerald, still in his pyjamas. When they had eaten, Jean led the three of them upstairs to a bedroom with a double bed. The sisters lay there in the dark in total silence. Years later, after the war, the three were reminiscing about that first night and asked one another what they remembered about it and each said, 'No one kissed us goodnight.'

Mr and Mrs Wills were always kind and treated the three sisters fairly and the trio will always be grateful for taking them in that night. Soon it became obvious that the three girls were too much for their hosts and it was agreed that

Joan, the middle sister should move next door with Mrs Jones and her daughter, Ruby. It did not matter really because the back garden was shared and they saw one another every day.

When Edna Goring arrived in Cornwall she and the other evacuees were given a medical before the selection process began. As she lined up she stood out from the other children, because her mother had dressed her in blue and the others were dressed in their drab school uniforms. Aunty Mabel, as she later called her, grabbed her hand and they waited as prospective foster parents walked up and down before around 100 children, trying to make their selection. Edna thought it was just like a slave market. When all the children had been chosen, one small girl was left standing on a table, with shoulders slumped and tears in her eyes. Nobody wanted her. Edna's heart went out to her and she asked, 'Aunty Mabel, can we please take her?' And she did.

Aunty Mabel's house consisted of two bedrooms, a living room and a kitchen. There was no electricity upstairs and they had to go to bed by the flickering light of a candle.

———◈———

A nice, friendly, slim, middle-aged woman who worked in the hotel stood before us and announced that the manager wanted to see the grown-ups in the bar but not the children. I followed Mum in and as nobody seemed to mind, I stood there holding my mother's hand while she held on to Billy. The manager was not a very happy man as he waved a piece of paper about. 'Ladies, here is a rota for you all to help run the hotel. A lot of my staff are in the forces and with what the government pay me I cannot keep most of my women on. You ladies will have to help.' He then went on to explain the duties and finished up by saying each woman was responsible for keeping her own room clean. He made it clear that he was not happy with the way the women had let the children run riot the previous night. There was a groan when he proposed that there should be a repair fund and I think he was asking for 3d a week. He also went on to say that in future the women would have to supply their own knives and forks.

After the meeting Mum took me upstairs and as she made the bed I could see she was annoyed by the way she thumped the pillows. 'Practically accusing me of stealing his knives and forks. I've never stolen anything in my life. I'm not staying here.' Thus began the hunt for somewhere else to go, which lasted ages.

Our first day was bright and sunny and we all went down to the harbour and sat on the beach. It was wonderful. The sun was shining and I took my first tentative steps into the sea. It was cold! The only swimming costume I had, if I remember rightly, was a pair of woollen swimming trunks which, when wet, fell down and I kept having to haul them up. I could not swim; in fact, I had never been in the water before and in my ignorance thought it was easy. So I ventured out until the water was up to my neck. Mum was worried and shouted out, 'Come here, Jimmy!' but she was too late as a wave swept over me. I spluttered, convinced I was going to drown. I turned and ran back for the safety of the beach but I was soon out there again; I was determined to swim, but never managed it until years later at Hackney Baths. The war seemed far away and in another land.

We walked to the next beach with the island standing tall and proud and I wondered who lived there. It was then that I saw the caves which wound their way under the hotel. At night, when all was quiet, the waves pounding underneath could be heard and I used to worry that the hotel might collapse to the shore below. One night, during the winter, a storm blew up. Outside we could hear the wind howling and under the hotel the waves were crashing through the caves. Suddenly all the lights went out and we were woken up and ushered down to the basement by candlelight, which threw deep shadows on the walls and ceilings. Gradually, it got light as we all stood round and by this time, Tony and I were fed up with doing nothing and so, when the grown-ups were not looking, we slipped out of the basement window into the garden. We stood up; it was a serious mistake. In an instant the wind caught us and hurled us towards the end of the lawn, with its 300ft drop on to the beach below. There was nothing we could do to stop ourselves as the wind swept us along. Luckily somebody had built a low wall at the edge of the precipice, which we slammed against and gratefully slid down, laughing as we went. We had no sense of danger but we had the problem of getting back to the safety of the basement, if we dared to stand up. Tony shouted, 'Do a leopard crawl.' I had no idea what he was talking about but Tony had seen it on the films and so I copied him and crawled on my stomach, with the wind battering my face, trying to push me towards the edge. Finally we got to the window; Mrs Parsons pulled Tony through and dealt with him with a clout on the backside. Mum was behind her, straining to get at me and when she did, I got a hug and the inevitable clip round the ear.

There were the inevitable rows. It had to happen with about twenty women and children living in close proximity. We were a class mixture. Some, like Mrs Snooty, were middle class while others, like us, came from the East End of London. We had one woman who was Australian. She had a boy about my age called Michael.

During the day she never punished him for anything he did wrong but saved any punishment till bath time. She would slash into him with a hairbrush. We could hear his screams all over the hotel and you could see the distress on every woman's face as his cries rang through the rooms. The women looked at one another, each wishing another would do something. Then, one night, Michael must have been particularly bad because his cries were louder than ever. Mum was seething. 'Hark at that poor sod. I can't stand it any longer, I'm going to sort the cow out.' With that, she flew up the stairs with the women and children in her wake, including Mrs Snooty. She reached the bathroom door, threw it open and stormed in, followed by as many women who could squeeze in. The women left outside cheered when they heard the Australian woman screaming as the rest beat her with the brush and their fists. Funnily enough, after that, we never heard Michael cry again! The women of the hotel had their own way of dealing with their problems.

—⚬⚬⚬—

During the war, despite rationing, Patricia Free never went hungry and, encouraged by posters to 'Dig for Victory', grew potatoes, greens and peas so they always had fresh vegetables. Her foster mother's father-in-law was a gamekeeper and would suddenly put his head round the kitchen door and hold up a dead rabbit by its ears. After school and during the holidays, Patricia would work on the farm to help supply the food.

For the second time since the war started, Marjorie Pascoe arrived back in Cornwall to live with her father's cousin in Glasney Terrace, Penryn. She had gone back to London the first time because, like so many, her mother could not see the point of her living away and putting their relations to a lot of inconvenience when she had a perfectly good home in London and nothing was happening. She soon fled back once the Blitz got underway. This time, instead of going all the way by taxi, the family went by train, taking her grandmother. On the way to the station the air-raid warning sounded and they rushed for the shelter. When the all clear sounded and they emerged, Marjorie was distraught; there was one fatal casualty – her doll! In the rush, someone had knocked its head off and it had rolled into the gutter and been crushed.

Her father's cousin's house in Penryn was in a row of four, with the toilet at the end of a long garden, which was terrifying at night. After a while, the house seemed very crowded and so Marjorie and her mother moved to Mrs Thomas' house. She had come down from London to live at a big house called Enys. She married the butler and, after a time, they left the house and opened a café in Redruth. Unfortunately, her husband heard the Americans wanted butlers and off he went.

Marjorie slept in a bed chair while her mother and grandmother slept in a double bed. After a while, Mrs Thomas opened a fish and chip shop. Marjorie was fascinated as she watched her preparing the fish but felt sorry for her in winter when Mrs Thomas' hands would turn blue with the cold. As the war went on, rationing hit everything and dripping became scarce. Soon, Mrs Thomas found she had only enough to open three days a week. She employed a schoolboy to put the potatoes through the peeling and slicing machines and sometimes she would allow Marjorie to do this. What Marjorie really loved was pushing the glass ball of the pop bottles against a peg and pressing them in.

The carriage on the train to Cornwall was crowded but Peter Butt and his brother, Tom, managed to sleep most of the way. The only thing he remembers about the journey was a porter at one of the stations shouting 'Parr! Parr!' which he thought meant the man had lost his father. It was dark when they finally pulled into Redruth station and Peter could not wait to get off the train. The weary children were ushered along the platform by people carrying torches as they struggled with their few belongings. There was no lighting in the station to fool enemy planes. Once outside, ten children were crushed into a large car but, luckily, they had not travelled far when it stopped and Peter and his brother were told to get out and were handed over to a Mrs Bluett. She treated the brothers well although she did not have the room. There were four boys and they all slept in the same bed, with Peter lying across the bottom.

A few weeks later, when their mother came down, she took one look and did not like what she saw and was adamant that her boys be moved. She was a very determined woman and, despite being told by the billeting officer that everywhere was full, she persuaded him to get Mr Mathews, his wife and his sister-in-law to take them. The three of them were in their sixties and were strict Methodists, with Mr Mathews being a lay preacher. They lived on a farm called Hillcrest in Sandy Lane, Carn Marth. Although they were not happy at having to take the boys in, they had to, because they had two spare rooms and under the law, if they refused, they could be hauled up in front of a magistrate and fined or imprisoned. It appeared that the boys had landed on their feet and their mother was pleased with her efforts but, unfortunately, it did not last long. Because they were elderly, the Mathews' found it difficult to cope with two young boys and so the brothers were split up. Tom went to Redruth and Peter remained behind.

Hillcrest had no running water but there was a standpipe just outside the gate. It also had corrugated barrels under the guttering of the outhouses around the farm which used to catch rainwater off the roofs. The house had no gas or electricity. Mr Mathews and Peter used a toilet in a shed, which consisted of a wooden plank with a hole in it, under which was a bucket. When it was full it was emptied into a pit in the garden. Toilet paper was the *West Briton*, cut up in squares and hung on a piece of string.

Left: *From left to right: Mrs Mathews, Aunt Eva, Tom, Peter and Mrs Butt.*

Below: *Tom and Peter Butt.*

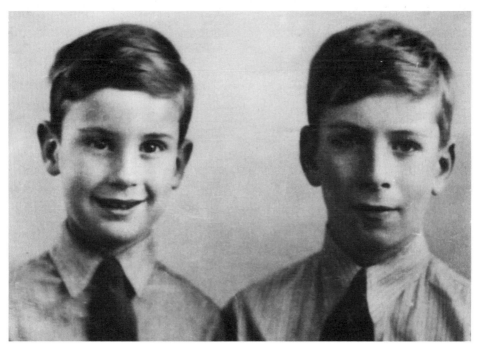

Saturday morning was always bath day. Mrs Mathews would fill the big copper urn with rainwater, taken from one of the corrugated barrels. The copper urn was built into the wall of the outhouse and a fire was lit to heat the water. When it was hot, Mrs Mathews ladled it into a tin bath.

The kitchen had a large oven range, which was black leaded each day. All the meals were cooked and eaten in this room, which was warm and dry throughout the year. Mrs Mathews would cook seven seedy cakes on Thursday and on Saturday, egg and bacon pasties.

Mr Mathews was always moaning about the 10s 6d the government gave him to feed Peter, but he more than made up for it by helping round the farm, collecting eggs and milking the cows. Every Saturday, Mr Mathews would ask Peter to take a covered basket down to Mr Ball, the grocer. He had to promise not to look in it and had strict instructions only to give it to Mr Ball. One day, Peter could not resist looking under the cover and was not surprised to find a chicken, eggs, homemade cream and butter from the farm. In return, no doubt Mr Mathews received a little more than his rations. Peter was horrified: was he part of the black market, acting as a runner? Uncle George, as Peter used to call Mr Mathews, was very strict and everybody was terrified of him.

Hillcrest, Sandy Lane, Redruth, 1944.

One day, Peter was pleased to learn that there were two other evacuees living just up the road. Their surname was Crawford and Peter often played with them but he was never allowed to do so on a Sunday, which was spent going to the Wesleyan chapel. On Sunday evenings, after church, the family would all go into the front room, which was the only day it was used. They would have supper and Auntie Mabel would play the organ and everybody sang songs in front of a roaring fire, which also helped to dry out the room which, like the rest of the house, was very damp.

Anne Vaughan and her sister were fortunate enough to have been billeted with Squire Johnson and slept in the servants' quarters. In the house were some mothers from the East End of London with their young children and they looked after the two girls. Not long after, they were moved to the squire's summer residence, Bodrigy House in the village of Cadgwith.

As the war drew to a close, people started drifting back to London but Anne and her sister stayed on until peace was declared. They had been so happy at Cadgwith and were reluctant to go back to London; Anne realized that she had spent more than half of her life away from her parents.

After thinking they were never going to be selected, Harry Drury, his brother, sister and the Howard boys followed Frances Smith, the lady in the Red Cross uniform, out of Mylor Bridge's village hall and into a large estate car, which impressed them. Frances drove through the countryside for about two miles and eventually stopped before a pair of great gates. Harry leapt out and opened them up and then jumped back in again. They drove along a long driveway to an enormous house. Outside, waiting to greet them, were the servants. One by one they were introduced to the butler, the cook, the maid Eileen Bell, and the estate manager Mr Joe Thomas. Harry's sister was told to go with the maid while the four boys were taken into the kitchen and fed with corned beef sandwiches.

They all thought they had landed in heaven. As they were led up to their rooms, the two Howard boys were given one room while Harry and his brother were put in another. At breakfast the next day they were told by the servants, 'You are never, ever to go down past the green beige door, they are the family's rooms.' After breakfast, the five of them were gathered up and went on a tour of the estate and were delighted to find they had their own private beach.

Harry Drury was lucky enough to be billeted to this magnificent house.

The Smith family had two daughters and two sons. The eldest daughter, Lucy, went in to the Wrens and the younger daughter, Susan, went to finishing school. The two sons were officers in the Army. Unfortunately, they were both killed, one parachuting into Holland and the other on exercise in Bournemouth.

In his hostel in Truro, Michael Duhig heard that his brother Billy was very unhappy and had made several attempts to get home to London by jumping on lorries. In the end, Michael's eldest sister and her husband came down and, for his own safety, took him back. Within six months, his twin brother, Paddy, who was missing him, followed.

The elderly couple, Mr and Mrs Hubber, who were looking after Paddy invited Michael to Sunday lunch and then, after a time, asked him if he would like to stay. He spent five-and-a-half happy years with them. They saw that he was well looked after and kept him smart. He was lucky enough to have a room of his own at the front of the house, with a double bed. It was sheer luxury. He still remembers the pasties and apple pies Mrs Hubber used to make.

Mr Hubber worked for the Great Western Railway and used to get chickens and eggs from one of his gang. The same member of his team also had ferrets and so there was often rabbit on the menu.

When the train from London pulled into the station, Elsie and Rose Bristol wondered where they were. They were none the wiser when the porter called out 'Truro'. They had never heard of it. There were no signs to indicate where they were and after taking a last look around the carriage to ensure they had left nothing behind, they alighted and were ushered along by one of the teachers. Outside, a coach was purring away patiently, ready to transport them to a school in Truro where they were given a cup of horrible tea, without sugar. They later found out that the sugar had been put into a cake they had been given. No sooner had they downed their tea than they were hustled out on to the waiting coach. The sisters were worried; it was getting dark and they were tired and weary. After going down country lanes they finally pulled up outside Crugmeer Village School. Inside, local people were milling about, waiting to select the child they wanted. Elsie was worried she would not be able to keep her promise to her mother that she would not let them be split up. A woman did try but they were determined to stick together. Suddenly, all the children were gone and the only person left was the lady in charge. They were worried and were wondering what was going to happen to them. Then the woman turned to them and said, 'You two are coming with me.' She took them to a little farmhouse where they were soon calling the owners, Mr and Mrs Pratt, Uncle and Auntie and were treated like family.

The two girls loved helping on the farm and were soon milking the cows as though they were born to it. The chickens were free range and they enjoyed picking up the freshly laid eggs. At harvest time they helped out with stacking up the corn and making the haystacks. Because they were on a farm they were well fed on vegetables, eggs, chicken and the odd rabbit. They had not been on the farm long when Mr and Mrs Pratt moved to a larger farm called Hillside and the sisters helped with the move as best as they could. One of the highlights that the sisters will always remember was when Mr Pratt took them out in the horse and trap. Elsie and Rose consider themselves very lucky to have had such good foster parents and even to this day, seventy years later, they still keep in touch with the family.

When the three Hanton sisters, Irene, aged eleven, Betty, aged nine, and Olive, aged seven, arrived at Penzance they thought they were going on holiday. They had travelled all day by train with Millbank Westminster School, having reluctantly left their mother and younger sister, Catherine, aged two, crying and ready to face the Blitz. Tired and weary, the three sisters came off the station and slowly climbed on the bus which transported them to the village of Madron, where they were ushered into Landithy Hall.

They stood in a line while people picked out the children they wanted. Betty's heart sank as Irene and Olive were selected by a Mrs Nichols, who lived near Madron Kennels. She had two girls of her own. Betty wondered if she would ever see her sisters again as she watched them disappear out the door. One can imagine how she felt as her sisters were taken off by a stranger. Finally, the person who owned Try Hall Farm picked her out. Reluctantly, she went home with them, wondering what had happened to her sisters. In the days that followed she missed them so much she felt sick. She felt alone and abandoned, and so she ran away. She was caught and brought back by the billeting officer and he moved her to Mr and Mrs Davy at Potteggan House, Rosehill, just over a mile from Maldron. To her delight she found out that her sisters had been moved to a farm run by Mr and Mrs Pollard, which was just across the way.

Mr and Mrs Davy had two girls, Trewey and Diana. Also in the house were two sisters, Margaret and Marion. Marion had a son, Humphry Davy, who emigrated to Adelaide, Australia. One of their ancestors, also named Humphry, was the famous scientist who invented the Miner's Safety Lamp in 1815.

At last Betty was happy; she had her own room and her sisters were nearby. What completed her happiness was that a dressmaker used to visit the house and made her a beautiful satin dress.

Monday was always washday, which took place in one of the outhouses. After the clothes were washed they were hung on the hedges to dry. The outhouse had a flush toilet and bath, which was unusual in those days. The house did not have electricity or gas and used oil lamps. One evening, they were sitting round the fire when they heard a loud bang. They rushed upstairs to find that a box of matches had burst into flames because somebody had left them too close to the lamp.

Irene and Olive loved living on the farm, which had cows, chickens, grew potatoes, beet and anemones. All the milking was done by hand and at harvest time everybody helped, feeding the threshing machine, stacking the corn and building haystacks. It was heavy work but the girls loved it. Unfortunately, Marion Davy became ill and could not cope with the girls. They heard they were going to be put in a children's home at Castle Horneck but at the eleventh hour Mr Joseph Pollard, who lived on a nearby farm, took them in.

Olive West (née Hanton) and her sister, Irene, loved being at Mr Pollard's farm, which was called Parc-an-Growes. It was constructed of solid granite and had a large kitchen with a long wooden table, fire range, larder and a window seat. Suspended from the ceiling was a gun rack with shotguns. There was a telephone with the earpiece attached to the side. The telephone number was PZ349. Olive remembers that you went upstairs to the three bedrooms but as you reached the landing you were greeted by a stuffed fox in a glass case.

Water was pumped up from an old well and lighting was by oil lamps or candles. The toilet was outside and everything went into a cesspool. Washing was carried out on a Monday in the old wash house with its copper boiler. There were a number of cows who were milked twice daily by the two sons, Bill and John, or by Donald Liddicoat, who joined the farm straight from school. Olive helped on the farm as much as she could, collecting eggs, feeding the pigs and pitching in at harvest time. There were a large number of cats and a sheepdog called Carlo.

For those not living on farms, food was scarce, especially as there was rationing. Professor Ken MacKinnon remembers the town crier, dressed in his ordinary clothes, ringing his bell round the streets of St Ives and broadcasting that a consignment of tinned food had just arrived. One of the items that was not rationed was fish and people would go down the wharf to buy it as it was landed, especially mackerel and pilchards. In the autumn, people would stand at the end of Smeaton's Pier as the sun was setting to see if any pilchards had been caught.

Ken thought the billeting officers had a really tough job placing everybody. One of them, Miss Braithwaite, had great difficulty placing Ella because she was black. Until the Americans came, people had seen few black people. Finally, Miss Braithwaite took Ella to Back Road West, where a lady took her in. That night when Miss Braithwaite was undressing Ella for bed, she found an envelope in her clothes. In it was a thank you note plus £20, which was a lot of money in those days.

In September 1939 Nancy Botterell, aged six, stood in Penzance station holding her mother's hand. She remembers her mother explaining why the evacuees were coming. They waited patiently as the train pulled in. The evacuees on the train looked tired, lost and bewildered as they clutched their few belongings. They selected a little girl evacuee called Doreen Stringer and took her back to Madron. Three weeks later, her mum and dad came down and took her back because the expected bombing had not happened.

After the tedious journey from London to Baldhu, Brian Little and his twin brother, Stan, waited in the school hall to be selected. After a while they were picked by Tommy Gill, who had been instructed by his father, a poultry farmer, to bring home two girls. Brian reasoned that they were picked by Tommy because, like them, he was a twin. On the first night at Belmont House, Brian looked out of the window, across the open fields, with not another house in sight and could not help comparing it with the busy street in London where the view from their Victorian house was just roofs of other houses.

Belmont, like most houses in Cornwall at that time, had no electricity. Each night they had to fill the paraffin lamps and trim the wicks. For water they had an underground water tank by the back door. The earth closet and tin bath were in a shed at the end of the garden. On washday and bath nights the old copper boiler was fired up with wonderful-smelling pine cones.

Brian and Stan helped on the smallholding and at night rounded up the chickens and got them into their large, Army-style huts to keep them safe from foxes. They had a really bad problem with rats who used to hide under the chickens, but would give themselves away by leaving their tails sticking out. Brian and the others would push the chickens out of the way and expose the rats, which ran for safety chased by the two dogs, which soon caught them.

In those days if you wanted a cow to mate, you took it to the bull. The farmer wanted to mate his cow, Daisy, and so he sent Brian to stand on the edge of the field to call her over and, to Brian's surprise, she came. One of the calves was called Stinker, for obvious reasons

The brothers loved helping on Church Farm, which had no tractors. Everything was done by big, powerful shire horses that used to plough the fields and pull the machinery. At harvest time the steam traction engine would puff away and drive the threshing machine, throwing out bundles of straw tied in the middle. Brian and his brother used to love to help stack these on to the horse and cart and help build the haystacks.

Tommy, the son, was very clever and converted a Dodge vehicle and trusted Brian to drive it. It was very useful for carrying goods about. Corn for the chickens was bought in a shop just up the road from Belmont. In a back room was a young blind man who used to weave baskets. Apparently, he lost his sight playing with explosives his father used in the tin mine.

Ellen Murt and her younger sister were fostered by Miss Hempsall, who was an old maid and lived in a house in St Agnes which, like most houses, did not have any modern amenities. Her middle sister lived across the road, while her brother, who was fourteen, lived up the road. Unfortunately, Miss Hempsall's youngest brother was very ill with a kidney infection and lived in a hostel.

Miss Hempsall was very stern and one day, Ellen's brother knocked on the door with a letter from their mother, but she would not let him in or take the letter off him. Another time they all went down to the beach and she went mad. It got to the point where Ellen could stand it no longer, and so they decided to ask the billeting officer if they could be moved. They could not settle down and moved several times. At one place, she was so bored, because all she had to do was sit in the garden and embroider.

At seventy-three, Mrs Sheila Nicholas never forgets sleeping on the floor of the Town Hall with all the other evacuees when she and her elder sister, Joan, arrived in St Just late one evening in 1940. Like a lot of parents, hers decided it was not worth sending them away in 1939 as nothing was happening. She was only five at the time and her sister was eleven. She was the youngest of ten children, with six sisters and three brothers. Couples had large families in those days; the invention of the contraceptive pill was twenty years away. The next day, in the Town Hall, the evacuees were given breakfast before the people came in and looked them up and down. She thought it was just like a cattle market. It was a wonder they did not look at their teeth! Eventually, a woman picked them out. Sheila found out later that they had only been picked because her name was the same as the woman's baby who had died.

The two girls had no complaints of how they were treated and had a wonderful time. The woman fostered three other evacuees; two of them were called Tony and Margaret, but they only stayed a short while and then, as frequently happened, their parents came down and took them back to London. Towards the end of the war, Sheila's sister reached her fourteenth birthday and left school and went back to London. There, she faced the dangers of the doodlebugs, with their distinctive engine noise, and later the V2 rockets, which fell silently from the sky.

Arriving at 9 p.m. at Truro station after travelling all day from Paddington, Reg Cook and his brother, aged six, were tired and weary but little did they know that their journey was not finished; they had another twelve miles to go. Reg helped his younger brother onto the bus and then sat back, hardly able to keep his eyes open. Finally, the swaying bus stopped and the evacuees, who could hardly put one foot in front of the other, climbed out and were ushered into the reading room, where the selection process took place. They stood there waiting, as child after child was picked. To his relief, he and his brother were finally picked by the local nurse. She was a glutton for punishment as she picked two other boys. Reg was so tired that he did not know where he was and did not care until the next morning, when he discovered they were on Treviles Farm, Ruan. As they sat at breakfast, the two brothers could not wait to explore. Once outside, they soon realized that they were living on a mixed farm of 131 acres. The house had a large entrance hall and five bedrooms. Their home in London would have been lost in it. One of its unique features was its flush toilet, which none of the other houses in the vicinity had, although it had no electricity. Cooking was done on a range, which was kept alight all day. Reg soon discovered that Ruan was only a small village with a few houses, but it did have a school, pub and one shop.

The boys will never forget Christmas 1941, when the farm was struck by an outbreak of foot and mouth and all the animals had to be slaughtered. They brought the police in and anybody who went in or out had to be disinfected. In no time at all, the disease spread to other farms in the area. The authorities carried out a thorough investigation and came to the conclusion that birds had brought it in. Once the infection was eradicated, the farmer, despite being disheartened, bought more cattle and gradually built up his herd once more.

If foster parents had children of their own, they sometimes treated the evacuees unfairly, especially when a quarrel broke out between the children. It was natural for some to take their own children's version of events. The biological children of the foster parents bore the brunt of strangers living in their home. It was the foster parents' children who had to share their parents' love and affection, their rooms and toys, and show the strangers, who might have a funny Cockney accents and different ways of living, around. So it was for Mr Wills, who was eleven when he stood at Wadebridge station waiting for the train to come in from London, loaded with evacuees. The train seemed never-ending and the platform was not long enough for all the evacuees to get off, so the train had to keep moving up. He watched as the children walked to the Town Hall, where people had gathered from the surrounding villages to take an evacuee home, trying not to split up families. The locals were shocked at the state of some of the evacuees who had journeyed from Wandsworth and Battersea; they were poorly dressed and looked undernourished. Out of their own money the locals bought them clothes from jumble sales, etc.

Mr Wills' mother walked up and down the line of children wondering which child would get on with her own boy. She picked one but she got it wrong and from the start the boys hated one another. Mr Wills junior was an only child and hated sharing his bedroom with the evacuee. They fought and quarrelled as the London boy thought Mr Wills was thick and Mr Wills did not trust this boy from the streets of Battersea. The conflict continued until the Londoner turned fourteen and went back to Battersea to work.

Unfortunately Mr Wills' peace did not last long, as one night, Plymouth was badly bombed and his parents took in a boy from there. He was a disaster and was always in trouble with the police, who were constantly knocking on the door for him. When the V1s and V2s started raining down, Mr Wills' parents took in more evacuees from Surrey. They were a great improvement on the others.

John and Fred Ellis, aged thirteen and ten respectively, were first billeted with Mrs Trip, who had a daughter living with her, but unfortunately there was a personality clash and so Mrs Trip's grandson, Norman, and his wife, Gladys, agreed to take the two boys in. They got on well and one day Norman took them out on a boat trip around St Michael's Mount. Unfortunately, Norman was seasick and while retching over the side he lost his false teeth. The boys remained friends with the family and each year exchanged Christmas cards. When John and Fred's mother died, they sent a tablecloth that their mother had embroidered as a memento.

In 1943, Norman and Gladys took in the Linley family, who were evacuated from the Elephant and Castle. The family consisted of Mrs Linley, Lois, aged nine, and Alex, aged five. Soon after they arrived, Mrs Linley gave birth to Jackie. Mr Linley came home on leave for a while to see the new baby but all too soon had to return to his unit.

Mrs Desforges sat in London wondering what was happening to her two daughters, Jean and Pat, in far away Cornwall. She was more worried about her younger daughter, as she knew her eldest could cope. But she had no need to worry because they had landed on their feet and had been selected by the local doctor's wife, Mrs Willis, and taken back to 1 Cross Street, Helston. The doctor had been a widower, his wife having died giving birth to their two daughters, Jennifer and Shirley, who were now at boarding school. He then married his wife's sister.

Jean and Pat soon became part of the family and were delighted to help Dr Willis with his baby son, John, and the older son, Jimmy. Jean and Pat slept in the attic, which at one time had been the maid's. The first night they could not sleep because they were very homesick and all night they could hear running water. Next day, they set out to find out the source of their annoyance and soon found it was the water, flowing down the street from the tin mines.

The evacuees loved the doctor's house, which was so much bigger than theirs in London. The playroom intrigued them. It was on the first floor and had a wonderful dolls' house. It kept them amused for hours, playing with the intricate pieces of cutlery and furniture. Another favourite place was the suite of rooms downstairs. The rooms had their own entrance off Church Street and, before he joined the Navy, were the doctor's surgery, waiting room and dispensary. Jean also started up a gang, who used to meet in one of the outbuildings and act out the radio stories of *Just William*.

Unfortunately, the good life came to an end when Mrs Willis went up to join her husband in Skegness and the girls had to move to another billet. At first it was suggested that they move across the road to a house where they had been to tea but they knew it was very depressing, restrictive and dirty. They fought against the move and won and were fortunate enough to move to Mr and Mrs Lismore, who lived just across the road. They had two daughters, Yvonne and Maureen, who were at boarding school.

Jean and Pat loved it, mainly because it had a huge garden. They were allowed to help the gardener, although they found the lawnmower hard to push. At first the Lismores had two maids, but soon they were called up and went off to help in the war effort.

Even today, the Lismores throw open their gardens and hold the Floral Dance. The gardens are enormous and have a boating lake. The public have a wonderful time, picnicking and dancing. There was an old iron pump, from which they pumped water up from a natural spring to use in the kitchen. Jean maintains that the water made a very special cup of tea and also remembers well tasting her first honeycomb straight from the beehive. The two sisters had a wonderful time, making carts, tipping over boats and climbing trees. By the lake, next to the cattle market, the Duke of Kent, who was killed in an accident in 1942, once came over and spoke to Jean and her sister.

Although there was rationing, the sisters never went hungry and if Jean didn't ask for seconds, they thought something was wrong. The local farmers always treated the doctor with produce when he went out to visit them if they were ill. Life in Cornwall gave Jean that healthy start in life which aided her in her career as an athlete in track and field events. She went on to represent Great Britain in the 1952 Olympics and many more international championships.

Madeline Fereday's (née Dunn) parents first took in two evacuees, Billy and Gwendolyn Brown, to their home in Troon. She thinks their father was a policeman. The two children were not very well behaved and caused problems. Madeline was very upset when Billy pushed in the eyes of her doll, especially as she had just received it for Christmas. Then he took the wheels off her doll's pram to make a go-cart. Madeline and her sister, Lillian, were so incensed that next time they were wringing the washing, they trapped Billy's fingers in the mangle. It did not damage his fingers but hurt his pride and taught him a lesson.

Madeline's mother had four children, plus she ran the village shop, and so when Gwendolyn and Billy became a problem, she asked the billeting officer if they could be moved to another family in the village. Mr and Mrs Prisk took Gwendolyn while Billy was taken in by one of Madeline's aunts, who lived at 18 Fore Street, which was at the other end of the village.

About a year or so later Madeline was playing in the garden at the front of their shop, which was a converted parlour, when she saw some children walking past with their luggage and the inevitable gas mask. They were accompanied by the local teachers. One of the children was black and at the school, when the children were being selected, families were reluctant to take him. The two girls asked their father if they could look after him and without another word, he went to the school. Eddie was standing at the end of the line, head down and looking very forlorn. The headmaster asked which child their father wanted and he pointed to Eddie and said, 'My girls want him.' Eddie fitted in well with the family. When his mother came down from London to see how he was she was delighted and then asked if they could find someone to take in Eddie's little sister, Frances. Mrs Dunn, Madeline's mother, asked her customers as they came into the shop if they would take Frances and Mr and Mrs Williams of New Street volunteered. Their father was a sailor and on a number of occasions he and his wife came down to see their children to the end of the war and then continued to come down for holidays for years after.

Madeline knew a number of families who took in evacuees: Norman and Enid Treblicock of Mew Street looked after Joan Greaves, while Vernon Transwell lodged with a local farmer called Lambrick who Madeline thinks farmed at

From left to right: Mrs Bull, Lillian, Madeline Dunn, Eddie and Mr Dunn.

the Lizard. Sadly Vernon's mother was killed in the Blitz. John Donahue, an evacuee, who lived near to the Dunns fell out of a tree in the local woods and was killed. He was only fourteen and lies in the same graveyard as Madeline's parents. Years later, they met his brother's wife, by chance, on the National Express coach to Heathrow.

4

PARENTS' VISITS

After the first great evacuation of 1½ million children, which commenced on 1 September 1939, everybody, including the government, expected the war to start in earnest. The government had ordered 400,000 coffins to cope with the expected Blitz but, except for some raids on the ports, nothing happened and people began to doubt if there was going to be any bombing of cities at all. It was called the Phoney War. Evacuees were writing home telling their parents they were homesick and what is more, parents were missing their children. Because of this, evacuees started to drift back home. Parents arrived at the evacuation centres and took their children home, even though they had to pay their fares.

When visiting the children who remained, parents were entitled to a monthly voucher to help with the cost of travel, provided they registered with their Local Authority. On the Great Western Railway, the demand was so heavy that they had to restrict the service to Tuesdays, Wednesdays and Thursdays, although they did run some special services at weekends.

―――

I had been in the hotel for about three months when surprise, surprise, Dad appeared! Mum did not know he was coming, he just turned up. That was typical of him. He wrote very few letters and Mum used to joke, although it turned out to be true, 'He's too busy with his other women.' When his letters did arrive, they had blue pencil marks through words the censors thought might help the enemy. Every letter that went out from a force's camp was read and, if it mentioned that the unit might be moving, the words were obliterated.

In the hotel they set aside a room for visiting husbands so that they had some privacy. From my point of view I found it difficult to adjust on the rare occasion he came home on leave because when he was not there, I thought of myself as the man of the family and tried to look after Mum. When he came home, I was naturally swept aside, which I resented. I don't think he was sensitive to my feelings or to anybody's, including Mum. He was in the Royal Artillery; so was one of Mum's brothers, Uncle Jim. They were in the same unit. He could have warned Mum of my father's affairs but I suppose it was difficult for him, seeing as my father was his sergeant and there remained a sense of honour amongst men. He said he was on embarkation leave but he never went. Apparently he had appendicitis and missed the boat. Uncle Jim must have been posted to another unit because many years later, I heard Dad tell Mum while I was 'ear wigging' that his entire unit had gone to Egypt and been wiped out. Whether he told her that for sympathy, I don't know.

While he was with us he did take us down to the beach and we had a wonderful time splashing in the waves; he even tried to teach me to swim, without success.

Newquay beach.

We played football on the sands with him in goal. I had never played before and he got annoyed because I did not know that I should not pick the ball up. When we tired of that, we explored the caves and the rock pools that had been left by the tide, trying to catch the small fish that darted about. We did manage to catch some small crabs. Each day he got up early and walked down to the local shops to get his paper. He would sit on the bed, light up a Woodbine cigarette and the first thing he turned to was 'Jane'. It was a cartoon strip of a young woman who normally finished up with very little on. Apparently the troops loved it but, at the time, I could not see what all the fuss was about. He was always moaning how the paper's size had been cut down since the war started. I learned later that his paper had been reduced from twenty-eight pages to eight because of the shortage of paper.

Soon he had to go back and, to be honest, I was glad, because I could get away with more. His harsh discipline was not there and once again, I was the man of the family. He had made quite an impression on some of the women at the hotel as some came out to say goodbye to him. I think Mum got quite jealous. He did not want Mum to go down to the station but she insisted. My heart went out to her as she kissed him and I could see the tears in her eyes. For days after she was very quiet and would sit on the bed and just go into her own little world. She realized that it might be the last time she saw him.

A few months after he had gone back, I was watching Mum and noticed she seemed fatter and remarked on it. In those days, nobody mentioned sex or babies and her reply was, 'I've been eating too much new bread.' Each day she got fatter and then one morning, Billy and I woke up and she was not there. Mrs Parsons came in with a very austere-looking woman and, taking both our hands said, 'Your mum's gone to hospital for a new brother or sister. She will be in there for about a fortnight.' In those days, women laid in bed for ten days after giving birth.

Mrs Parsons dressed us and packed our battered suitcase. Billy and I looked at one another and wondered what was going on. Nobody had explained. The thin, serious woman took our hands and led us, or rather pulled us, out of the hotel. 'While your Mum is having the baby you are going into our home.'

We thought we were never going to see Mum again. We walked through the streets, breathing the cold morning air. It was October and a mist hung over the sea. We walked for what seemed to us like hours. Finally, we climbed the steps to a big house with bay windows. A straight-faced man opened the door, grimaced and, taking our hands, led us down to the basement where about four or five other children of various ages, from thirteen down to Billy's age, looked up from having their breakfast, grunted and then continued eating. We had not had anything to eat but we were not invited to join the other children. Mr Austin took our hands again and took us up the steep stairs, which seemed to go up and up. Finally, we reached the top and, for a moment, stood on the landing while Mr Austin took out a great bunch of keys and opened one of the two doors. Inside, there were two beds and, without a word, he turned and left the room. I froze as I heard the lock in the door turn; we were shut in. Billy started to cry, 'I want my mum.' I put a brotherly arm round him although I felt the same as him, but being the eldest I could not show my feelings and upset Billy even more. We had to escape and get back to the hotel, but I did not know how to open the locked door. Billy cried but finally fell asleep with exhaustion. At about midday I heard the thump of footsteps on the stairs and the key turn in the lock. It was Mrs Austin with a plate of sandwiches and a cup of tea.

'If you can behave you can come downstairs.' When she left I noticed the door was left unlocked. Billy and I sat on his bed, scoffing the sandwiches as we planned our escape. We were invited down for dinner but afterwards were sent straight back upstairs. That night we lay fully clothed on our beds. Nobody came up to see if we were alright. When I judged everybody had gone to bed I shook Billy and whispered, 'It's time to go!' I remember him slipping off the bed, looking really tired. Carrying our suitcase we crept downstairs, determined to find Mum. Each time a stair creaked, we stood stock still and waited for someone to come out, but nobody did.

The staircase was pitch black but somehow we reached the bottom and felt our way along the passage to the front door. Through the fanlight window, the moon threw a beam of light onto the floor. Finally we reached the door and, with relief, I turned the handle and pushed; it was locked!

I looked up and could just make out a bolt, but how to undo it? I signalled to Billy to stay where he was and made my way to a room on the left. Inside, I saw a pile of chairs stacked in the corner. With care, I lifted one off and carried it out to the front door and climbed up. The bolt was just out of reach. I stood on my toes and stretching up, my fingertips touched the bolt. The next thing I knew I was falling. My arms flayed out as I tried to find a grip but failed and went crashing to the floor. I lay there winded while Billy started to run up the stairs, only to meet Mr Austin coming down. He grabbed him by the ear and led him down to me. I rose from the floor just as he lashed out and caught me round the face. There were no questions asked; he knew we were trying to escape. Marching us up the stairs, he threw us in our room and as he locked the door he shouted, 'You'll get no breakfast for that!' Later, as we lay on our beds frightened, he opened the door and threw our case in.

He kept his promise, and we had no breakfast and he did not bring anything to eat until lunchtime. Just as it was getting dark, he came in and grabbed Billy and started cramming his clothes into a carrier bag, all the time holding onto his collar. Finally he pulled Billy towards the door as he screamed at the top of his voice, 'It's the last you'll ever see him!'

Drawing myself up to my full height I demanded, 'What you doing with my brother?' He laughed, a laugh I will never forget. 'I'll teach you to run away. You're troublemakers. We're going to split you up!' With that, he slammed the door shut and locked it. With tears running down my face, I hammered on the door, shouting, 'Leave my brother alone!'

There is nothing like hunger for subduing the spirit. Later that night, Mrs Austin came in with two sandwiches and a glass of milk. She sat down on my bed and, putting an arm round me, tried to explain that it was for my own good.

Billy's birthday was on 13 October and, to my surprise, Mrs Austin asked if I would like to see him. I was still hurting over being split up; after all, we had been constant companions since he was born. We set off through the streets, stopping at a sweet shop for something for Billy's birthday. Sweets were on ration and it was difficult to pick out something he would like. Finally, I made my choice and we were on our way again. I was worried that Billy had settled down in his new home and that seeing me would upset him. Mrs Austin knocked on a large door and it was opened by somebody who could have been her sister, tall and skinny. I had made up my mind. I would not see my brother. It would upset him too much. I explained it to both the women and they looked at me strangely; they did not understand. Mrs Austin was annoyed. 'We've come all this way and now you don't want to see him? I don't understand.' After giving the woman the sweets, I walked down the steep steps and looked back, tears streaming down my face and there in the window was Billy, crying. All these years later we still talk about that day and the hurt that we felt, although we are both now in our seventies; he weighs seventeen stone and has done manual work all his life and is one of the strongest men I know, but the thought of that time still upsets us both.

One day, all the boys in the home, about ten of us, were taken by Mr Austin to the local park to play football. I played right back, whatever that meant. The only time I had played football prior to this was on the beach with Dad when he was on leave. I did not have a clue about the rules, other than you had to get the ball in the net. Somebody kicked the ball to me and I turned and kicked it at the goal and scored.

Fancy, in my first game, scoring a goal! I threw my arms in the air, delighted and could not understand why nobody else was enjoying my triumph. You had to get the ball in the net, yes! But nobody explained there were two nets and I had scored an own goal. I was never picked again and I have always hated the game ever since.

In the home there was only one thing to do, bearing in mind in those days there were no televisions or record players and at the Austins' we were not allowed to listen to the radio, which only left a jigsaw puzzle of the Union Jack.

Finally, the day arrived when we were taken home. Mum greeted us with a bundle in her arms; she was cuddling our brother, Fred. I must admit I had missed Mum and was jealous. Mum must have realised it and sat me down and put this little bundle in my arms, with the instructions, 'Make sure you support his head.' Looking down at him, I was not impressed. He was crinkly, had very little hair, cried a lot, especially at night, and he smelt; he has changed a lot since then.

⎯⎯◈◈◈⎯⎯

Frances Bishop was split up from her sister and it was inevitable that as time passed, being in different schools and homes, they saw very little of one another. Their parents did write to them regularly. When their father had a long leave, he would make the journey down from London and take them to their favourite place, Carn Brea, and they swam in the sea at Portreath. He would go back happy in the knowledge that his daughters were safe and healthy.

John Glyn was very homesick at first, as were most evacuees. He even thought about walking back to London, but eventually settled down, especially as he and Clive Rogers became friends following their selection together. Revd Price and his wife kept his parents informed of his welfare. One day, he had a nice surprise when his father and brother visited him out of the blue. Both wore their Home Guard uniforms but they only had one gun between them and no ammunition. Their visit was followed by one from his mother and elder brother, who had exchanged his Home Guard uniform for a Royal Air Force one and had just finished his training. Soon after, his brother was sent abroad and finished the war in India.

Stan Mason was five when he was evacuated and two years later, when his mother came down to see him, he did not recognise her. To him she was a total stranger and he fled. Finally, he climbed a tree to get away from her. It was not long before she won him over but the incident must have upset his mother.

Carn Brea, 1944.

Sheila Sells was delighted to have been selected by Mrs Eddy at Sancreed School. Mrs Eddy was only twenty-two, and took Sheila to her parents' farm. There, Sheila was thrilled to have her own room but had to give it up when her parents came down to see her. She had to sleep in the bath, but she did not mind as she was so pleased to see them after such a long separation.

The house was like many in Cornwall at that time; it had no running water and water had to be fetched from a stream, on a trolley, from just beyond the farmyard. Sheila became an expert at fishing tadpoles out of the water before they used it.

Sheila Nicholas' father was in the forces and successfully applied for a transfer to Bodmin so that he could be near his daughters. He was so keen that he used to hitchhike to St Just and would arrive on all sorts of vehicles, anything he could hitch a ride on, just to spend a few hours with his daughters before he had to go back. If he had been late back he would have been in trouble. On one occasion Sheila was going to chapel when he arrived unexpectedly. They were talking when, suddenly, a bomb dropped close by. They rushed to the church but the door was locked.

The journey to Cornwall from London was long and expensive, even though the parents were given cheaper fares. Many evacuees did not see their parents for the six years until the war ended, but most kept in touch by letter and, of course, there was the excitement of the parcel at Christmas.

Communications were not like they are today. Very few people had telephones, mobile phones had not been invented and nor had emails. Jean Pickering was lucky because her mother sent her a parcel each week of clean, ironed washing and a little treat. Every week, Jean and her sister took the parcel of dirty washing down to the Post Office and sent it back to West Ham. It would weigh 15lbs, which was the maximum they would take in those days, and it cost 1s 3d. Her mother managed to do this all through the Blitz even when, because of the bombing, she had no gas or hot water. She would then boil the water up on a fire. The amazing thing was, although it was wartime, nothing went missing in the post.

When the Blitz appeared to be over, Jean's mum finally come down and took them back to London. Her elder sister, Joan, was due to marry her fiancé, Anthony, who was a flight lieutenant in the RAF, but one terrible day she received the dreaded telegram stating that he had been killed while on a bombing raid over Germany.

At first, Betty Hanton and her two sisters, Irene and Olive, hated being in Cornwall as they were split up. Once Betty was moved near them, life changed and all three began to enjoy their stay. They had travelled down to Madron with their school but left their very young sister, Catherine, behind in London.

The girls' parents visited as often as they could at weekends and brought their young sister with them. One weekend, while they were visiting, a bomb was dropped in a field nearby, which made a great crater. All the local children were all over it, looking for shrapnel. One of the locals looked at Betty's dad and then at the crater and said, 'The Germans must have followed you all the way down here from London.' Betty also remembers the sky raining down propaganda leaflets.

In London, during August 1940, the raids got so bad that Betty's parents decided it was time for their daughter, Catherine, to be evacuated and join her sisters in Cornwall. On the train down they suddenly found they were in the middle of an air raid and Saltash Bridge was hit. The train could not go any further. They were transferred to a coach and made the rest of the journey in it. When they finally arrived in Cornwall, tired and weary, they still had to find a place for Catherine. They struck lucky and found a couple in Madron,

Madron Church and School.

not far from her sisters. All weekend Catherine cried for her parents. In the end the couple became worried that it might make her ill. They knew that the sisters' parents were leaving that night. They rushed down to the station with Catherine in their arms and were just in time to see Catherine's parents getting on the train and handed her over. Catherine went back to the carnage in London to take her chances.

The father of Mrs Jones (née Mitchell) was a headmaster of a school near Redruth and had over 100 evacuees allocated to his school. For a very short time her parents also had two girls billeted with them but as they got off the train in Truro there was a raid and the hospital was bombed. When they wrote to their mother they must have told her about it. She was on the next train to take them back to London as she reasoned that Truro was as dangerous as London at the height of the Blitz.

Not long after, her parents took in two boys from London and they stayed right to the end of the war. Then, one night, the Germans bombed Plymouth and left it in ruins. Evacuees from the stricken city came streaming out to the safety of the countryside. Mr and Mrs Mitchell felt sorry for them and took in another boy, who was only five years old.

Yvonne Watson's father was a GP and took in two girls from London, Barbara and Pamela. They were very lucky to be alive, as a bomb had landed on their doorstep and wrecked their house. They only stayed for a short while and then went back to London. Soon after, her parents took in two more girls, who stayed with them until the war ended.

Peter Butt was in Cornwall when he heard that his father, who was a policeman in Bow, London, had been awarded the Police Medal for exemplary service. He had rescued a large number of people from bombed buildings and, on one occasion, had helped to recover over 300 bodies from buildings that were not far from where his wife was sheltering.

Peter's parents took it in turns to visit him and his brother. On one occasion, his father was on his way back to London when his train was suddenly stopped. As he waited there he must have wondered what was happening. Later, he found the reason for the delay was because Plymouth Docks were being bombed. It took him eighteen hours to make the journey to London and in all that time he had no food or drink.

Whenever Peter's mother came down he knew it meant a visit to the shops with her clothes coupons in hand, to buy clothes for him and his brother. What Peter liked when either came down was that they spent time with them, taking them out to one of the seaside towns.

5

SCHOOLING

The Anderson Committee did not give sufficient attention to the detailed planning of schools. It is not surprising really, when you consider all the other items they had to plan for. It was the biggest evacuation this country had ever known, it never having been done before, and therefore, with no model to go by, it was hardly surprising they got some of the details wrong. The Committee's idea was that the reception areas' schools should absorb the influx of evacuees. No consideration was given to any spare capacity the local schools might have. Some teachers from evacuated areas went with the children from their school and were meant to fit in. It would appear that little thought was given to the equipment the children would need when they arrived, nor to the differing standards of education. Some reception schools were able to cope with the influx, but many could not, and additional schools were set up wherever room could be found; village halls, church halls, anywhere where desks, chairs and blackboards could be set up. In some halls, only curtains divided classes so it was difficult for the children to concentrate. In the author's school in Newquay, like in many places, we spent half days at school and the local children did the other half. Children's education suffered but I suspect that the main objective of the Anderson Committee was to get the children away quickly to a safe area and for local authorities to sort out what they considered was the lesser problem. At least the children were safe!

—⟨⟩⟩⟨⟩—

When I first arrived at the Great Western Hotel, there was no mention of that word most children dread – school. In the East End, every child was expected to hate school or there was something wrong with them. I was not very good at it and found things difficult, but I loved it, and was big enough not to be bothered by the bullies. As there were so many of us in Newquay, the local authority set up a special school in an old wooden hall. Later, some of the local children joined us. We had one teacher, who taught all age ranges from five to eleven. The classroom was not set out in rows, where the teacher stood in front, but the desks were arranged in an oblong. There did not seem to be any formal teaching, as I remembered it in Essex and London after the war, but there were a series of books round the room, hanging from hooks, and the idea was that you started at the beginning and worked your way to the end. There were no checks, and once you had looked at the first book, you moved on to the next. A competition developed, and we all raced to finish the last book. We were totally unsupervised. We did not understand the contents of the books and we were left to our own devices. I have come to the conclusion since that the authorities were just going through the motions with us. They had to provide education. There was a shortage of teachers – most of the men had joined the forces – and they could at least claim they were giving us some form of education.

There had to be a day of reckoning, which for us meant a test; it was not surprising that most of us failed. The teacher suddenly realized what we were doing and so I was back on the first book, but this time I was tested before I moved on to the next.

The teacher took us out on wonderful nature walks along the cliffs and on to the beaches. I can remember the fresh sea breeze blowing in my face and, I now suspect to keep us occupied, her pointing out various birds and animals as we walked along. Although she did not instil much knowledge into me, she did implant a love of nature which has lasted all my life.

I don't know if it was the war or mothers going out with the local soldiers, which many of the women did, or that many of the local children came from farms, but the children were obsessed with sex. They talked of nothing else and in the playground would simulate the act. After school, they would go out in a crowd on to the grass or beach, out of sight of the grown-ups, and would all try and have sex. The teacher found out, but did not know what to do, and so she did nothing. It would have been better if she had given us sex education lessons, but in those days I doubt it was part of the curriculum. I have often wondered how many of the girls became pregnant when they reached puberty.

As we were so far from the danger zones we had no shelters that I can remember, and one day, suddenly, the siren went off. We kids from London knew what it was and in the absence of the teacher telling us what to do, we dived under the desks, where the teacher joined us. To us, it was a laugh. Hitler had had his chance in London and if he did not get us there he was certainly not going to get us in Cornwall. Anyway, it turned out to be a false alarm.

Soon after the incident of us failing the exam, another teacher was brought in who seemed to have more ideas; she actually used a blackboard and taught about the British Empire, with which she was obsessed. We used to have a third of a pint of milk a day and, as the biggest boy in the school, it was my job to bring in the crates of milk. I did not mind that, but there were children almost as big as me and I felt they should take their turn. At dinnertime, I helped the two teachers to move the table to one side and put up trestles. Why we did that, I don't know, only to me it would have made sense to have our lunches on the desks, but the teachers were the bosses. Over the tables we rolled out linoleum from poles. I had heard artillery firing one morning and it must have been playing on my imagination for, as I was rolling up the cloth after lunch, I kept poking the poles through the cloth saying, 'The guns in the desert, bang, bang.' I was ordered to stop, but I must have felt in a rebellious mood, as I kept on. All the other children were outside playing, where I thought I ought to be. The elder of the two teachers went in and got the cane and then threatened me with it, but I still persisted. They then bolted the door so I could not get out, and then chased me round the room, striking out at me with the cane. Each time I passed the door I leapt up, trying to pull the bolt back, but every time they were right behind me. Finally I dived under one of the desks and they caught me. I was thrown across the desk. They pulled down my trousers and, in anger, slashed into me while I screamed at the top of my voice. When they had cooled down they stopped and, sobbing, I pulled up my pants and made a final leap for the bolt and opened the door.

All the way back to the hotel I sobbed and when I got there Mum was sitting in the dining room with some of the other mothers. She leaped off her chair and screamed, 'What's the matter?' Between my tears I gave her my version of what had happened. She did no more than pull my pants down in front of all the women. Mrs Parsons said, 'You're not going to let her get away with that, are you, Lou?' Mum's face went red, her temper was up and the teachers were for it!

On the way out, Mum snatched a cane from one of the dahlias in the front garden and marched determinedly towards the school, waving the cane. Every time we came to one of the women from the hotel, down would come my trousers, exposing the wheals on my bottom. I felt my trousers were going up and down like Tower Bridge. We reached the school just as the children were coming out. Each child looked in awe at Mum, as she brandished the cane. She swept into the classroom with me following in her wake, and roared, 'What have you done to my

Jimmy?' The two teachers backed away. Mum pursued them. 'He deserved what he got,' said the younger of the two. It was not the right thing to say to Mum at that moment. She swished the cane, so that it came within inches of the younger one's legs. 'How would you like it? He was only trying to help and what do you do? Beat him! You vicious cows! I've a good mind to report you!'

They tried to explain what happened and Mum began to calm down. 'You're lucky my old man's not here, he'd knock your block off! If you touch him again, I'll do it!' With that, she took my hand and led me outside where all the kids had been listening. After that, I was a hero at school and was never told to do the tables or milk again.

Later in the war teachers asked us what size shoes we took and, soon after, we went into school and there were wellington boots piled up in the corner. Apparently, the Americans had sent them over to children in the country. As shoes and clothes were on ration, Billy and I wore them every day until our feet were sore.

One day, one of my friends, Billy Foster, did not come into school and we wondered why. We all thought he was ill. Then rumours started to spread that his father had been killed. When, some weeks later, he returned to school he was very quiet and not his normal self. He used to be the one who was always playing tricks but now all he did was to keep away from everybody. Gradually it came out that his mother had come down to see him from London and told him his father was missing. Apparently, his father had been in the Army in Egypt. Billy was never the same after that and it brought the war home to us.

—◦◦◦—

Marjorie Pascoe was enrolled in the local Church of England school at Penryn but was not prepared for the hostility of some of the local children, who thought all Londoners were ruffians. Although she did not have a Cockney accent, they treated her as if she had. She was determined to blend in and used to sit in the toilet trying to perfect her Cornish accent, but she went over the top and spoke broad Cornish, which was just as bad. She must have worked hard because today she is accepted as Cornish.

Frances Bishop and her two sisters, Joan and Pat, went to school soon after they arrived in Cornwall. Her two sisters went to Barncoose and she went to Pool, but there was a lot of bad feeling between the locals and the evacuees. At their separate schools they all had to endure resentment from the Cornish children, as they were seen as intruders, and were called 'dirty evacuees!' On one particular day, in Carn Brea playing area, she was playing on a slide which was very popular with the local children when she saw a local boy bullying one of her sisters. He was big enough to hurt Frances, and kept calling her sister 'a dirty evacuee.' Frances was normally a placid girl but, brave as a lion and without a thought that she might get harmed, she hurled herself at the bully and pummelled into him. She gave him a good thrashing and he went home crying. She did not know who was more surprised, him or her, but he left her sister alone after that.

Towards the end of 1942, Frances sat her eleven-plus at Pool Methodist Church. After taking it she forgot all about it until one day in February 1943, she went to school as usual and was summoned to the headmaster's office. Mr Pascoe, or Beaky as they called him, was a good teacher and encouraged the children in music, drawing and painting. To her surprise, he told her she had passed her eleven-plus and, as a result, would have to go to a new school. When she asked where, he replied, 'Buckinghamshire'. She was stunned and did not know what was happening but the headmaster was delighted. Then she thought about her promise to her parents and said she could not go, because she could not leave her sisters. The headmaster smiled and said, 'Don't worry, it's all sorted. Your parents know all about it.'

'When do I go?' she asked.

'Tomorrow,' he replied. When she arrived home her case was packed and very early the next morning she set off, on her own, with her sandwiches to her new school in High Wycombe. Nobody had thought to let her say goodbye to her sisters.

John Glyn had a different experience of school in Newquay in that it was spasmodic. The first one was over a garage, with a small coal-fired stove at one end where the teacher stood, warming his back. The folded tables were set out in fours. During that first winter of 1940, the children were so cold that they were allowed to wear their coats, hats and scarves and when it got really cold, they wore balaclavas. He cannot remember any of the lessons or if he learnt to read or write there.

Edna Goreing had to share the school with the local children and they took it in turns. One week the local children went to school in the mornings and in the afternoons the evacuees went. When the children started drifting home, because of the very little bombing in the cities, the children integrated and finally did full days at school.

Mrs Patricia Free had a similar experience of sharing days at school, going afternoons one week and mornings the next. She kept busy when she was not at school because she used to pick peas and potatoes and used to stack hay on White's Farm in Madron. She earned 16s a week, which was good money in those days bearing in mind that when she left for work two years later, she earned only 10s 6d at the Co-op.

Stan Mason's fellow students in Constantine's school were not very interested in the three r's and made very little effort to learn, but if you asked them how to catch rabbits on a moonlit night or look after chickens, tend cows, sheep or any farming question, they were a fountain of knowledge. He found it a culture shock when he was transferred to another school. It was right at the top of a steep hill which Stan had to climb each day. In winter, when it was icy, it was even more difficult as he took one step forward and two back, so consequently he was always late. The headmaster, Mr Wonnacott, did not understand and used to give him six of the best every time. Stan's father, who was in the Royal Artillery, was given a temporary posting to Falmouth. Stan told him about the caning and he went mad and said, 'Leave this to me, son.' He marched up to the school and, putting his face in Mr Wonnacott's, he growled, 'If you cane my boy again I'll come back and shoot you.' His father must have frightened the life out of the teacher because he never caned him again.

Some of the boys from the East End of London were very poor and a number of them went to school without shoes. One boy called Maurice was one of these children and thought that being evacuated to Cornwall was the best thing that had happened to him.

The three sisters, Irene, Betty and Olive Hanton used to go to the school in the village of Madron. Some of their teachers from Millbank Westminster School were evacuated with them, which made the transition from London to Cornwall easier. It meant their education was not interrupted and friendships formed in London were kept alive. On Sundays, the friends would meet up at church, which was next to the school.

Not many of the evacuees took an interest in the Cornish language but Ken MacKinnon did. The London County Council School for the evacuees in St Ives was in what are now the church buildings in St Andrew's Street. There were two classrooms in the same hall divided by a curtain. The headmistress was

Miss Wellock, a large, bosomy lady with red hair and, as Ken puts it, terrifyingly severe glasses. When he arrived at the school he was made to stand before her and recite his times tables and, as a result, was allocated to Miss Tregale's class.

Miss Tregale came with them from London but originated from Cornwall and inspired Ken with tales of Cornish legends, of Giant Bolster, of the wicked Tregeagle baling out Dozmary Pool with a leaky limpet shell and taught him to sing the adopted Cornish national anthem 'Trelawny'. She read the children stories of Brer Rabbit and *Wind in the Willows*. She also brought in outsiders to teach the children about their specialist subjects. One person she brought in was an art teacher who taught Ken to draw the old Smeaton Lighthouse and said, 'You start with a pickle jar!' The local children in the school were divided between those who treated the evacuees with indifference and the others who did not hide their dislike.

Ken MacKinnon did not only go to school but, along with other evacuees, attended Barnoon Sunday School, which was run by Mr Martin. They also met for Bible classes on weekday evenings, which were held in the basement of Mr Martin's shop in Fore Street. There was emphasis on Bible reading but they did have one very irreverent evacuee who, every time 'synagogue' was mentioned, asked, 'Well, what about goosegogs then?'

The hymns were displayed from a roll of sheet suspended from the ceiling and were sung with gusto, especially anything to do with the sea. One day, they were given a party, and people must have given up their rations to supply the food. When Ken goes back today he can still see the spread set out. He is still remembered and is welcomed by the people who knew him, like his Sunday school teacher, Gaffey Williams, and his grandson, Richard Farrell.

Mary Garnham went to Sancreed Church School, which was about four miles from Penzance. It had only two classes, which was very different from the Senior Street School in Paddington. Sancreed Church School was where they brought the evacuees from Penzance by coach for selection and she was lucky enough to be picked by Miss Mabel Wherry, an unmarried woman living with her parents. Mary and her sister stayed with them throughout the war and they got used to living in a farm cottage with oil lamps and candles for lighting and calling Miss Mabel's parents Grandma and Granddad.

Sheila Sells also went to Sancreed but had to cross six fields to get there, pushing the cows out of the way as she went. Before she started school she had to help

Cows grazing.

with the milking and collect the eggs in the hen coop. As she climbed the steps to the hen house she would take a stick and hit every step to frighten the rats. After school, she had to herd the same cows up and used to pick up a fern and hit the last cow on the backside, to make it move faster. Sometimes, as a treat, she would be taken to school by pony and trap.

At school there were a number of evacuees but many got homesick, or their parents missed them, and they went home without warning the school.

It did not take long for Eileen Penwarden to become friendly with the children in her school; many of them had gone to the same school as her in London. As was typical at that time, they had mixed classes in the infants and junior school but when they got to the senior school, the young adults were separated. She found the lessons easy and did not think the standard was as high as she had been used to, but perhaps this was due to the war and the fact that many teachers were now in the forces. Despite this, she took her eleven-plus and passed, but not many did.

Sheila Nicholas and her sister thought the teachers at the school she went to in St Just were wonderful. They were Miss Simpson, Miss Richard and Mr Vinnicombe. In contrast to many of the other schools, the locals and the evacuees mixed well; in fact, so much so that she is still in touch with some of them all these years later.

Mr Clark was pleased when his elder brother and his two sisters, Thelma, aged eight, and Gladys, aged thirteen, were evacuated with him from Edmonton to St Just. He and his brother stayed at Little Darren Farm, which was owned by Mr Prowse. His two sisters were at a farm nearby called Darren Farm, owned by Mr John Pearce. They all went to the same Kalynack school and mixed well with the local children. Miss Ross and Mrs Harvey were the two teachers who were good but Mr Clark did not learn much, except drawing and painting. The influx of evacuees must have put a tremendous strain on teachers, schools and resources. He thinks that, given the circumstances, the teachers did a wonderful job.

Some of the children who were evacuated on farms were given extra time off during harvest and Mr Clark helped to gather in the corn, stacking it up and helping to load the horse-drawn carts with bales of straw. It was hard, tiring work, lifting the corn with pitchforks. In the corner of the field would stand the steam-driven threshing machine, with its ever-revolving belt from the steam engine. All the ploughing was done by great horses. The children would help with the backbreaking work of pea picking, bending over and plucking the pea pods of the plant into sacks which were weighed by the foreman to see if somebody had slipped in stones to make up the weight. Potato picking was just as tiring and at the end of the day one would go home tired and hungry, but full of fresh air. Many children, like Mr Clark, were given tasks to do before going to school, like milking the cows and feeding the chickens. The evacuees on the farms learnt a great deal.

Harry Drury and his brother had to tramp about two-and-a-half miles across the field or sometimes they would take the easier route along the road to Tremaine Hall, which had been set up as a special school for evacuees. They had three classrooms and a teacher for each room. The head was Mr Wilkinson, who was assisted by his wife and also Miss Dale. She later married a French lieutenant who sailed across from France in a small boat.

Before Reg Cook went to school he had to carry out certain duties on the farm. He was up at 5.30 a.m., put on his old clothes and he and another boy had to milk the three cows by hand. After that, he fed the five pigs and the chickens. Then it was time for breakfast and finally he washed and changed before walking down the village to the school. In summer, he had a green card which meant he was given an extra twenty-five days off school to help with the harvest. At first, the local children called them names and then, gradually, they got used to these strangers from London. For about eighteen months he went to the village school and then, for some unknown reason, they closed it and he was transferred to the larger school called Veryan. Sometimes he walked the four miles across the fields to his new school or, on other occasions, he caught the bus at the top of the lane. The school had three classrooms but the toilet was outside and consisted of a hole in the ground with a plank of wood across. At the end of the day, lime was thrown down to cover the contents.

The education was basically the three r's but the discipline was strict, with liberal use of the cane and ruler. Reg thought that one of the teachers, Mr Bennett, was very good and fair but if he stepped out of line he received a clout with the ruler.

For six-year-old Peter Butt, school seemed a long way, especially in the wet weather. On their way to school, the two Crawford boys, who were also evacuees, would call for him. At Trewirgie School in Redruth the classes were large but, as evacuees drifted home in 1942-43, they became smaller. Like many children at that time, his education had been interrupted and, as a result, he had difficulty in spelling and had a complex about it. He dreaded the practice of the teacher going round and asking each child to spell a word out loud.

After a time the local boys accepted him, but never enough to let him play in their football team. In 1944, more evacuees arrived to escape the V1s and V2s and challenged the local boys to a game of football. He tried to join the evacuees' team but, because he now spoke with a Cornish accent, they did not want him. There was some bad feeling between the local boys and evacuees. The locals would gather on the South Down and then march up to Carn Marht armed with sticks and stones. Peter and his friends would wait on top of one of the old mining tips and, as the enemy advanced, hurled stones down at them. Surprisingly, nobody seemed to get hurt. If they were driven off the tip, Peter and his gang would run down to the sheds on the farm.

Michael Duhig noticed that as the war went on his school classes in Truro became smaller and smaller as evacuees went home, until they were left with only one teacher, Miss O'Sullivan. In the end they amalgamated with another evacuee school and Miss O'Sullivan went with them. The school had two teachers, Miss Anderson and Miss Furness, and they had three classes. Michael really enjoyed school, especially the walks through the countryside and the music lessons, where they sang songs like 'Little Brown Jug', 'Riding Down to Bangor' and 'To Be a Farmer's Boy' from the *Forty Song Book*.

She only attended her school for a few weeks before Jean Pickering was transferred to West Ham Secondary School, which was a long way to travel each day, but when war broke out the whole school, including some of the teachers, were transferred from London to Helston Grammar School in Cornwall. Everything from the school was moved except the building, but they overcame that by having their morning lessons in the church hall in the High Street before all trooping down to the school itself in the afternoon. Although you had to have coupons for clothes, the school kept the same uniforms. Helston Grammar School had large playing fields and the evacuees made good use of them, including having many great games of rounders.

Ian Blackwell and his sister, Heather, joined the local village school at Gorran Haven which took children aged five to fourteen. In the school there were a lot of London evacuees who were rough and ready. The teacher who taught the twelve to fourteen-year-olds was Mr Vivian, who also taught his daughter. The school was pretty primitive and had no mains water, but there was a large overhead tank in the grounds with a hand pump. There was a rota for the boys to get the water each day and Ian said he liked doing it.

His schoolroom was heated by a big iron stove, which glowed red hot. On top of the stove was a tin box in which the local farmers' children heated their pasties. One day the paper wrapped around the pasties caught fire and the children all made a grab for their cindered lunches. When it rained, and they could not go out in the playground, they would stand round the fire and spit on it to watch the moisture sizzle. To help the war effort, and teach the children about gardening, each was given a patch of land to cultivate vegetables.

On the way home, Ian and his friends would make knives from flint and cut off chunks of swede and chew them. The old school burnt down and Ian often wonders if there was another pasty fire. Let us hope that the new school has a modern heating arrangement!

Whilst in Kent, Anne Vaughan passed her eleven-plus and went on to Tonbridge Wells Grammar School but when she got to Cornwall, it would appear that her success had been forgotten and she and her sister, Jill, were sent to the village school in Ruan Minor.

Stennack School in St Ives had sandbags at the front entrance and Mr Gribble remembers Lois and Alex, two evacuees who were staying at his parents' market garden, who got up to all sorts of mischief like playing truant and hiding under their special bush until school had finished. One of the worst things they did was to play with matches under the bed, nearly causing a fire. The boys loved searching for shrapnel in a bomb crater in one of their fields. One day, the three of them were picking blackberries when Mr Gribble reached up for some berries at the top of the bush when he fell and badly gashed his leg.

There was trouble at Baldhu School, where Brian Little went, between the evacuees and the locals. The authorities decided the only answer was to separate them. They moved the evacuees to an outbuilding of the vicarage opposite, but first they had to carry out repairs. They had to put in a new wooden floor and then roof trusses, which were red, and so the school became known as 'Ruddy Beams'. It was freezing in winter, despite the heat thrown out by a Dutch oven on which they heated their pasties.

Kea School, where Clive Mathison went.

Shirley Downs remembers the large numbers of evacuees attending her school at the Voluntary Primary, which did impact on their education. There were six classes, three upstairs and three down. One of the rooms was very large and had a curtain dividing it. Shirley found it very distracting, especially if the lesson on the other side was more interesting. During raids, they had no shelter, but sat in a little room while one of the teachers told them a story. She remembers one teacher, Mr Tonkin, who came down from a school in London. He had apparently originated from Cornwall.

Many schools were cobbled together to accommodate the influx of evacuees. Although Ken Foxon, who went to St Ives, considered himself lucky to have some of his own teachers from London, their school was makeshift and had only one room, which was divided by a curtain. The children found it very disturbing, as they could hear the lessons from the other side of the curtain. If that was not enough to contend with, the local branch of the St John Ambulance was in the hall above. They only went to school for half a day, alternating between mornings and afternoons.

When the air-raid siren sounded, the whole school trooped down to the cellar and sat round a piano, singing songs until the all clear was given.

6

RUMOURS ABOUND

There were rumours of spies everywhere. It was said they would sneak into some of the quieter beaches along the coast. Frequently, after being out to play till late, we would see the Home Guard patrolling the cliffs and assumed they were looking for small boats landing with spies on board. They, the Army and police would set up roadblocks without warning, throwing barbed wire across the road and stopping anybody travelling along it. If you travelled on one of the single-decker buses, a policeman would suddenly appear, stop it and climb aboard, asking everybody for their identity card. Everyone, except children, had to carry one. There were notices and posters up such as 'Careless Talk Costs Lives', 'You Never Know Who's Listening' and, one of my favourites, 'Tittle Tattle Lost the Battle'.

We were also aware of the enemy within. We had been warned about it at school and on the wireless. As children, despite the war, we would travel for miles, often pretending to be Africans, running in bare feet and carrying spears. One day there were about four of us, and we discovered a river. There, half-hidden under the hanging branches of a willow tree, was a house boat. We had never seen one before and stretched temptingly across to it was a wooden plank. With my friend Tony leading, we stepped across it and climbed over the rail onto the deck and peered through the window. There, standing over a primus stove, was a very fat man, his stomach hanging over his trousers. He wore a grimy grandfather vest. He was a spy; we were convinced! As we turned to get off the boat to report our findings to the police, David, one of the gang, knocked over a broom which was leaning against the cabin and the man looked up. His face contorted and he shook his fist and it was obvious he was going to capture us and sail back to Germany. Tony shouted, 'Run!' and we took off. For a fat man, he could move and we were only halfway across the plank when he stepped on it. We thought he was going to kill us. As we ran, he shouted at the top of his voice at us in a foreign tongue – or was it our imagination?

Once on the bank, we ran like rabbits and soon outstripped him. With my lungs bursting, I looked back and could see him wobbling along, his stomach swaying from side to side. We did not stop running until we could no longer see him and then, gasping for breath, we burst out laughing. We would be heroes; we had uncovered a spy ring! Instead of going straight to the police, who we thought would not take us seriously, we decided, after a council of war, to go home and tell our mothers. At first, they did not believe us, and laughed, but we insisted. 'Honest, Mum, he was a spy. He spoke gibberish!' At last, we convinced them and Mum used the hotel telephone to tell the police.

In those days, there were no mobile phones. Very few homes had telephones and normally you would have to go out into the street to phone. We did not get a telephone until the 1960s. Anyway, Mum telephoned the police and a very stern-looking constable arrived and was ushered into the dining room, where the four of us all tried to speak at once. Nobody wanted to miss the tale and all the mothers and children gathered outside the room, trying to listen, and all wanted to be in on catching the spy. The policeman held up his hand and told the rest of us to shut up while Tony told him what happened. Halfway through, he smiled, but let Tony carry on and then, finally, he said, 'You've done well lads, but unfortunately, he's no spy. We know about him. He's Polish, came over when the war started. Wanted to join up but he was too old.' We were all disappointed. We hoped to get our names in the paper as the spy catchers.

We did not get a lot of enemy action but one night there was bombing in Plymouth. The Germans wanted to try and knock out the docks and some of our Navy. As we lay in bed we heard the aircraft droning overhead. It was funny how soon you were able to tell the different sounds of the engines and Mum would say, 'Don't worry, boys, that's one of ours. Come on, let's get down to the basement.' It did not happen often, but on this occasion Mum said it was one of theirs and in our night clothes, with our winter coats wrapped round us, we joined most of the hotel in the cellar. I don't know why we thought it was safe as the caves were under us and if a bomb dropped we would be entombed by the hotel falling on us.

Suddenly, we heard the guns blasting away and out of the kitchen window we could see the tracer shells streaking through the air and the searchlights lighting up the clouds as they swept the sky, seeking out the enemy bombers. There was a loud explosion and Mum screamed at us, 'Get away from the window!' Although we were not a target, the German planes would jettison any bombs they had not dropped on the target on the surrounding countryside, so they did not have to carry them back across the sea to Germany. Later in the war, in Wickford in Essex, my grandfather and I would stand on the veranda of his bungalow and watch the planes returning from their raids on London. In the distance, the sky glowed from fires in the docks. Many bombs dropped harmlessly on open countryside, but some did not.

One of the prize possessions for us children was shrapnel. One or two of my mates had picked up pieces in London and, when their mothers were not looking, would take a dirty, old piece of rag containing a piece of shrapnel out of their pocket and proudly show it off. The piece was normally jagged and it was a wonder they did not cut themselves on it.

To increase our credibility within our gang, Tony and I decided we must have a piece of shrapnel and the bomb or bombs that the Germans dropped that night was too good an opportunity to miss. Sneaking some bread from breakfast and putting water into a milk bottle and stuffing the top with paper, Tony and I set out without telling our mothers.

Not only children hunted for shrapnel.

We did not know where the bomb had dropped but we heard somebody in the hotel saying they thought it was over the golf course, so we set off asking people we met where the bomb had dropped. Most did not know. Some made a wild guess, while others were sure it had fallen near the golf course and so we headed in that direction. It was a beautiful day, the sun was streaming down. We took our shirts off and threw them over our shoulders. Finally, we met a platoon of soldiers who were out on exercise and were lying exhausted on the ground with their rifles and equipment scattered around. At first, I was reluctant to speak to them but Tony was not as shy as me and went up and asked, 'Do you know where the bombs fell?' They were very friendly and asked, 'Why do you want to know?'

I could see Tony was reluctant to tell them and so I piped up, 'We want to get some shrapnel.'

'Wait till you get old enough to be in the Army, then you'll get plenty.' One of them gave us a bar of chocolate, which was a rare treat. Tony and I shared it but I saved a bit for Billy and put it in my pocket, where it melted.

Refreshed with the chocolate, dried bread and water we set off again in search of shrapnel. The soldiers had given us a good idea where it was, or so we thought. We had been walking for some while and were both tired. In front of us we saw a great house and Tony dared me to knock on the door and ask where the bomb had fallen. With reluctance, and a lot of foreboding, I walked up the long pathway. The door was opened by somebody very much like Mrs Austin, who looked down on me and asked, 'Yes, what do you want?'

'Do you know where the bombs dropped? The soldiers told us they dropped them over this way.' She looked at me suspiciously, and then took my arm and pulled me into the passage.

'Why do you want to know?'

'My mate and I want to get some shrapnel.'

It was beyond her comprehension that anybody would want shrapnel; she had no idea how highly sought after it was. She led me into what appeared to be the dining room, where old people were just sitting around and there was a strong smell of urine. Another woman who was younger came in and the woman who looked like Mrs Austin explained what I wanted. They looked at one another and the older one said, 'Wait here.'

I felt I was in trouble and I wanted my mum. The woman came back and said, 'I've phoned the police. Now tell me who you are trying to find out for.' I stood there, terrified.

'Nobody, Tony and me wanted to get some shrapnel, honest, miss.' I thought I had better call her that, for she was just like a teacher. Somehow, that convinced her.

'You can go now.'

'What about the police?' asked the other woman.

'I didn't really call them. I wanted to see this boy's reaction.'

I could not wait to get out and when I did, Tony was nowhere to be seen. He'd rushed back to tell my mum that some old lady had abducted me and I met her halfway back. She gave me a hug, then a clip round the ear. She put her hand in my pocket to get out my handkerchief to wipe my face and discovered the melted chocolate. I never did get a piece of shrapnel, but I did get another clip round the ear!

7

ENEMY ACTION

August 1942 was warm and sunny and most of the evacuees in St Ives were on the beach, including Ken MacKinnon. The children were doing what all children love to do when given sand and sea; they were damming the stream outlet on Porthminster with sand, only for the water to burst through, while other boys were digging trenches, pretending there was going to be an air raid. Suddenly the siren sounded, but the children ignored it because there had been so many false alarms in the past. As a plane flew over, the children waved. Then, to everyone's horror, they recognised the crosses on the wings; the plane was German! The aircraft circled overhead flying back and forth and then, suddenly, it swooped down low, enabling Ken to see the pilot just as the machine guns opened up, sending spurts of sand in the air. The evacuees dived in the trenches they had dug, while others crouched behind the rocks, praying. The plane flew on and the children stood up, amazed nobody had been hit. For days after the children searched the beach for bullets in the sand but none were found. Ken found out later that the plane had been attacking the local gasworks. When he got home he found his landlady in hysterics because a bomb had hit the local cemetery and killed a lady.

After the bombing, Ken found Miss Perkins taking revenge on a picture of Naples Bay with a chopper. Up to the time of the bombing, Ken suspected that there was some admiration for the Germans locally as, before the war, von Ribbentrop had been a popular visitor to St Ives, but the raid destroyed that.

We were lucky that in Cornwall, apart from the area being loaded with soldiers and airmen and the Germans dropping the occasional bomb on their way back from Plymouth or Falmouth, most of us felt reasonably safe from the ravages of war.

One day Mrs Acton came back from visiting her mother in Plymouth. I heard Mum say she thought she was lying and that she was not visiting her parents but seeing a sailor. She had left her two boys, Clive and George, with Mum. Clive was about my age and we got on really well. She should only have gone for the weekend but as she had not returned by Monday, Mum got us all ready for school but when she collected us, she told Clive and George that their mother had not returned yet. I could see Mum was worried

There was still no news the following day. Then we heard on the grapevine that the docks at Plymouth had been hit. That night, after Mum had got the other children to bed, we were sitting in the bedroom when there was a knock on the door and Mrs Acton came in. As soon as I saw her, even at my young age, I knew something was wrong. Her face was as white as gloss paint and when she saw her two boys, she grabbed them and cuddled them to her.

'Lou, you will never believe it. I nearly got killed. It was a close thing I can tell you. Mum lives, or did live, near the docks. I just got in after going to the pictures when all hell let loose. The old siren started and I grabbed Mum, she's seventy-three, and made her go in the Anderson shelter. Admitted, it was a bit smelly down there and there was about half an inch of water, but thank God we did. We lay on the bunk beds, listening to the bombs falling outside. Suddenly there was such an explosion, the shelter shook and I got out of bed and paddling through the water, I peeked outside. All I could see was clouds of dust and debris. As it cleared, I could see that the garden was covered in Mum's house and in the distance I could see the flames leaping up from the docks. We stayed in the shelter, terrified. I didn't tell Mum what I had seen, but she guessed. After what seemed hours, the all clear went and when we got outside, and Mum saw what remained of her house, I thought she was going to have a heart attack. I'm sorry, Lou, to lumber you with the kids for so long, but I had to sort Mum out.'

'Why didn't you bring her back with you? She would have been safe here.'

'The council fixed her up with a flat and helped her move in.'

Again, the war had been brought to our doorstep.

Soon after this incident all of us, Mum and my two brothers, went down to the harbour and were sitting on a seat, watching the boats sway at anchor and seagulls fly overhead when suddenly a Spitfire skimmed overhead with flames streaming from its engine. I could see it was going to crash as it got lower and lower to the sea, just touching the waves and then, with a splash, it was down. We watched in horror, wondering what was going to happen to the pilot and praying he would escape. To my surprise, the plane still stayed afloat and a figure emerged and stood, waving. It was always a joke with us that the lifeboat took forever to launch. We had often watched the crews pushing the boat down the slipway and if the tide was out, across the sand. To our dismay, we noticed the tide was out. The crewmen raced down to the boat but suddenly there was a roar and, looking down, I saw *Splinter Bird*, a speedboat we boys always admired, hauling up her anchor. The two-man crew were running around the deck, making ready to go to sea, and then it was off, bouncing over the waves. I could still see the airman standing on the wing, waving his arms. In no time, *Splinter Bird* was alongside the plane and the pilot was on board and heading back to the harbour. By this time, the news had travelled round the town and a big crowd gathered, and as the speedboat came in a loud cheer went up and everyone surged forward to catch a glimpse of the airman. Unfortunately, when I looked down at the beach below, I could see the crew still struggling with the lifeboat on the sand.

There was great excitement in the hotel. There was going to be a parade through the town, in aid of the war effort. All the children were so excited that their mothers could hardly control them. I remember walking down the hill and seeing flags and bunting fluttering all along the road and the crowd was a sea of colour as people waved Union Jacks. We children were pushed to the front but nothing seemed to be happening as we waited and waited until, suddenly, we heard the swirl of the pipes and I strained to see and stepped out in the road. There coming towards me was a pipe major throwing his mace into the air, his kilt swinging as he marched. I had never seen a man in a kilt before and, although I was awestruck, I thought it was strange. Behind him came his pipe band unit, their kilts swinging. With the wail of the pipes and the sound of the drums, I was entranced.

People moved through the crowd with buckets, collecting money. Mum had given us each a silver threepence piece and, reluctantly, I put it in the container, for as Mum said as she handed it to us, 'It's to help win the war so that Daddy can come home.' Being the man of the house, I remember being not too keen on that!

Behind the pipers came Bren gun carriers, a type of armour-plated car which was low to the ground and had tracks instead of wheels which made a clinking noise as they turned. Sticking out was a Bren gun and each carried three or four soldiers with their rifles between their knees. In the distance I could see a lorry but could not make out what was on the back. As it drew level, I could see the model of a frigate in battleship grey with sailors in their blue uniforms and blue and white hats bouncing round the edges of the lorry. Everybody cheered, many no doubt remembering the battleship HMS *Hood* which had not long gone down, sunk by the Germans. Then came more squads of soldiers, their boots crunching in time on the road, their rifles at the slope. I could not wait to grow up and be a soldier and fight the Germans; I hated them! All too soon the parade disappeared into the distance and, reluctantly, the crowd slowly dispersed, all hoping there was more to come. After that, it seemed that it was an annual event, but I am not sure.

After school we would have a typical tea of bread and jam, swilled down with tea, which always seemed cold and very weak. Mind you, there was rationing and you could only have 2oz of tea a week. You could have 6oz of butter or margarine a week, but not both; you could only have one or the other. Cooking fats were rationed to 2oz a week but people would use the fat off the meat and melt it down. I used to love dripping, especially beef. Some people thought the shopkeepers were taking advantage of the shortages and storing food up to sell on the black market. In those days there was no such thing as teabags; tea was made in a pot with tea leaves. Tea remained the English's main drink but 2oz did not go far. When Mum made tea, she would boil up the old tea leaves until the tea was black. She would then dry out the tea leaves and reuse them. It was a horrible cup of tea!

Directly Mum released us after tea, the gang would meet outside on the wall, waiting for everyone to turn up. There were normally five or six of us and we would play football, which I hated, or cricket, which I also disliked, or rounders, which I loved. We had the makings of male chauvinist pigs because, if we were short, we might let the girls play. Some of the older ones were better than us, but we did not like to admit it. We would play until it grew dark, when we were called in for a bath and bed. Frequently we would wander off and watch the Home Guard and regular soldiers drilling on the cliff tops, waiting to repel any German invaders. If they did come, we all swore we would obtain knives and guns; God knows from where, but we would help the soldiers defend our country. One evening on the cliffs, we watched fascinated as we saw what we thought were commandos fighting with knives. They were paired off and one had a knife, a real knife, while the other tried to take it off him.

We cheered when one of the commandos threw the other and disarmed him. Their sergeant (he had stripes on his arms) told us to clear off, or words to that effect. We had all heard the words before in the hotel when the women argued. We moved beyond a hedge but soon we crept back, inch by inch. When we forgot ourselves and cheered again he chased us off, but he soon got fed up and left us alone.

One Saturday we all took bread and jam, plus a bottle of water, and set off on an adventure. We had no idea where we were going but, again, there were about six of us. The Snooty kids asked to come but we had banned them long ago when the eldest boy offered round a bottle of lemonade. There are no prizes for guessing what it was, but it did not taste very nice and I felt sick after. On the way, Tony cut some sticks. He was the only one with a knife and we set off, chanting in what we thought was African. We sang away in the hope that some of the words might be right, the law of averages and all that! We pretended the sticks were spears and we were going to hunt lions. Where we got the idea from, I don't know. We threw the stick in front of us, practising for when we saw a lion. The scenery was wonderful. On one side was the ever-moving sea, topped with white curling surf, and on the other were green fields. Then, as if by magic, before us were the banks of a river, but no water. We found out later it was the River Gannel. In the distance, we could hear the sea. As few of us had seen a river before, not even the Thames, we plunged down its banks and, in single file, we walked along the damp river bed. We had discovered the Nile.

Chanting as we went, we ignored the people picnicking on either side as they gazed down on us. Suddenly, somebody shouted, 'Look out, the sea is coming in!' I looked at Tony, who shrugged his shoulders and we carried on towards the noise of the sea. Again, the man shouted, waving his arms. We looked at one another thinking he was mad. A woman started shouting at us, then we heard the roar and coming towards us was a great rush of water. Abandoning our sticks, we rushed to the bank, trying to climb up, as we heard the water getting nearer and nearer. People ran towards us, offering us their hands and pulled us up, just as the water swept inches below our feet.

'You silly little buggers, you could have been drowned!' shouted one of the men. I turned and looked down at the swirling water as it swept past us and realized how lucky we had been. After that, we went back many times to look at the water and I wondered if I could outrun it but luckily I never put my running skills to the test. We were lucky that we never heard the ghostly cry of the crake, which cries out to lonely strangers.

—◦◦◦—

Edna Goreing remembers many of the hotels being taken over by the forces to house the wounded, including the Atlantic. As the men recovered, they were frequently seen round the town in their blue uniforms; unfortunately, many were badly disfigured. The Atlantic Hotel, high on the cliffs, was commandeered by the government and housed wounded troops. Everybody was expected to do their bit to win the war.

One day, a bomb dropped in the road, throwing up mounds of earth and making a great crater. Edna's sister came to visit her from London and wondered what all the fuss was about. After all, it was only a crater and in London it was a common sight, there were hundreds. It was thought that the bomb was meant for the docks at Falmouth but the German pilot must have missed the target and jettisoned it before turning for home. Falmouth was an important town in the war effort as many oil companies had supplies stored in the West Country, including 48 per cent of the Royal Air Force's oil. In 1941, during one of the attacks, a bomb fell within 25ft of a tank and 172 gallons of fuel was lost. A further bomb fell and a fire started but the burning oil flowed into the crater of the first bomb and did not set the rest of the tanks on fire.

One day, she was walking along the road when she heard a plane flying low and did not think much of it until it started firing. Bullets started striking the pavement and everyone ran for cover; some cowered in doorways and others lay flat on the pavement while machine gun bullets struck the ground all around them. It was a miracle that nobody was hurt.

The Atlantic Hotel.

Some time later, she went to visit the docks and started talking to some sailors and invited them home: she was only seven at the time. The sailors were only about eighteen and probably had little sisters and that is why they took to her. One of the sailors, named Roger, gave her a book which he signed 'With love, Roger'. She still treasures it to this day. As people were away from their families, they did things to help others, hoping that somebody might do the same for their sons or daughters.

Mrs Patricia Free stayed in Madron and remembers seeing the Home Guard and was very proud of the fact that the uncle of the woman where she stayed was a colonel in it.

In those far-off days you never knew what was going to happen. Dave Thompson was playing in a field near where he was billeted when he saw a small cylinder in the wet grass. Curious, he bent down to look at it. During the war, children were warned not to pick up any metal objects because the Germans dropped containers specially designed to tempt children to pick them up. If they did, they exploded. He was sure it was a pigeon container and so he picked it up and, after carefully unscrewing the cap, was surprised to find two sheets of paper, held together by a hair clip. Slowly, he unrolled the paper, only to find a note which he thought was written in French. Wondering what to do with it, he asked two ladies from the village. They shook their heads and one of them said, 'The squire will know, he's in the Home Guard.' Taking him by the hand, they led him up to the squire's house. He looked at it, shook his head and kept the papers. Dave was still wondering what was written on the paper when the local policeman knocked on the door. Much to his surprise, he was not arrested, but was shaken vigorously by the hand and thanked, but he never found out what was written down.

When Nancy Botterell was six she heard the wail of a siren going off. All the family crowded into the kitchen to crawl into the Morrison shelter, which was just like a large table, made of steel with sides of wire. As a child, she thought it was always a long time before the all clear sounded.

All was going well at Cliff Farm, near St Just, until a bomb dropped in one of the fields. Although it was not funny, Sheila Nicholas could not help laughing because one of the cows got covered in mud, but luckily was not hurt. The next night, there was another raid and bombs were dropped on St Just, and two people were killed standing outside a shop.

She says that although most of the beaches were protected by barbed wire, there were places one could get through to the sea. She could get down to the sea from Pendeen Lighthouse.

On one occasion, when Sheila Sells' parents came down, they all went for a walk. It was just getting dark and bats swooped low overhead. They climbed a hill near Penzance and sat down at the top, watching the sea. Suddenly, in the distance, they saw the white clouds tinged with reds and yellows; Plymouth was being bombed. It was like a fireworks display. They sat in silence, watching the spectacular scene before them and thinking about the poor people being bombed.

Her parents took her to St Ives one day, which was the only beach open as all the rest were strewn with barbed wire to prevent the Germans landing in the event of an invasion.

Not all the bombs dropped on Cornwall were German and Sheila remembers getting up early one morning and watching as our planes skimmed across the tops of the waves after returning from a raid over Germany. In horror she saw them jettisoning their remaining bombs harmlessly into the sea. Sometimes the bombs would overshoot and land in the fields.

One night, there was an enormous crash and the windows were blown out. A German bomb had dropped and blew up the pigsties, throwing pigs' muck everywhere.

As she stood in the window Eileen Penwarden could see in the distance that the whole sky glowed with colour, a sure sign that Plymouth was under attack.

Later, some soldiers took over a mansion in Mevagissey, not far from where she lived. She also remembers the Ghurkhas being stationed near them. When she and her brother were returning to London with their parents, Eileen remembers sitting in a carriage with two Ghurkha officers. Her brother was fascinated by their turbans and took his father's scarf and tied it round his head, without much success, until one of the soldiers smiled, took the scarf off him, and showed him how to do it. They could all not help laughing.

Reg Cook remembers an enemy plane coming down at the top of the lane in Ruan and the excitement it caused. All the children from miles around converged on it in the hope of collecting souvenirs, but when they reached the plane they were disappointed; their way was barred by soldiers.

A searchlight at the Cornwall War Museum in Davidstow.

A few stray bombs dropped on the farm fields around, but one night he and his brother stood in the window and watched the sky light up with searchlights as they sought out the enemy planes. When they found them, the ack-ack opened up and they saw the tracers winging through the night sky. Then they heard the heavy thump of the bombs as they fell on Falmouth Docks. It looked like an enormous fireworks display.

At one time, they had four airmen billeted on the farm and their job was to set lights around the isolated parts of the area to deceive the German planes into believing that something important lay below, so that they would drop their bombs harmlessly in the mud.

In the village of Ruan there was no normal siren warning. The farm was one of the few houses which had a telephone and so, when an enemy aircraft approached, the telephone rang and gave the farmer the warning. He would step outside and blow a whistle, which would be taken up by the whole village.

Because John Reid was very young he was evacuated with his mother and sister to a farm near Mevagissey. However, it was not suitable and so, after consulting the billeting officer, they were moved to Gorran Haven, where a Miss Hurrel took them in. The house was called Gwineas and overlooked the harbour and the Gwineas rocks. They all slept in one room and had the use of the kitchen. Life was very good until the war caught up to them with a vengeance. They frequently heard the ack-ack firing at the German bombers returning from bombing Plymouth or Falmouth. One day, they saw a German plane on fire, heading straight for them. They crouched down, holding their breath, waiting for the impact. Then, they heard the roar as it skimmed over their chimney and crashed in a ball of fire in a field just beyond their house.

On a separate occasion, John and his sister were playing on the beach at Gorran Haven when they saw a German fighter bomber coming towards them, skimming the crest of the waves. Suddenly it opened up its machine guns. People scattered everywhere. Somebody threw John under an upturned boat and as he looked out, he breathed a sigh of relief when he saw the plane fly up the valley. Then, to his horror, it returned, firing as it came. John thinks that there were some casualties. When the German planes jettisoned any bombs they had not used on their raids on the docks, they often seemed to think that any target was fair game – including children playing on the beach.

Ellen Murt was shocked to hear the news that a woman she knew who went shopping in Padstow was wandering round the shops when the air-raid warning went and everybody rushed for shelter. She heard a bomb explode nearby and she prayed that her family were safe. Sadly, when she got home she found her house had received a direct hit, killing her husband, son and mother.

Ellen used to do some housework for a woman who sometimes used to give twelve American airmen a meal. She was devastated when she heard they had all been killed in a bombing raid over Germany.

When Ellen left school she started training as a nurse at Bodmin Infirmary. One day, while she was out, the warning went. She heard an explosion and when she looked across at the hospital, she could see it had been hit by a bomb which killed a number of people

When the drone of enemy planes was heard overhead and the sirens wailed, everybody ran for cover. Most of the raids were at night but there were occasional daylight ones. Mr Clark and some others were working in the fields when, without warning, an enemy plane swooped down and started firing at them. They threw themselves behind a stone wall and could hear the bullets bouncing off it. Where they had been standing just seconds before, great chunks of earth flew in the air.

One day, a company of soldiers commandeered one of their barns and started cooking a meal. In a corner was a tin of grease, which the soldiers grabbed. They quickly started frying their bacon and eggs in it, not realizing it was axle grease.

Like many parents, Mr Clark's came down after the bombing had stopped in London and took him and his brother and sisters back, but he liked it so much in Cornwall that he did not want to go.

Shirley Downs saw the sky light up as the Luftwaffe bombed Plymouth. At night, people would leave the city and move out to the countryside to avoid being killed and then go back to work in the morning. A few bombs dropped around Bodmin but mainly they fell harmlessly in fields. One family were not so lucky; they were having a reunion when a bomb came through the roof and killed most of them.

Shirley's family did not have a shelter and when the air raid warning went off, they all ran along the back gardens with their heads down to a communal one which was not properly kitted out.

One day, Harry Drury and his sister were walking along the side of a hedge towards a camp that they had built behind a bungalow. They could see two of their neighbours, Mrs Thomas and Mrs Young, talking in front of the property. Suddenly, they saw a plane circling overhead and then, without warning, heard cannon shells smashing into the hedge. Harry threw his sister to the ground and lay protectively across her, while the shells rained down. He heard the women screaming, but after the raid he was relieved to find nobody had been hurt.

One night, there was a raid on Falmouth and two ships were bombed and badly damaged; one was called the *Tusca Lusca*. A number of men working on the ships had been killed and the following morning the ships were still burning. One had a cargo of jute. They were towed out into St Ives Bay, where one of them was sunk. The *Tusca Lusca* became stuck on a sandbar and was there for months while they worked on sealing up the compartments.

One day, Harry was playing on the beach when he became aware of the sound of an aircraft getting louder and louder. Suddenly, the ack-ack opened up and all the earth shook. He saw the plane catch fire and, as it got lower and lower, he could see the cross on the side. He thought for a moment it was going to crash into the sea but at the last moment, it lifted its nose and flew over the headland and crashed in St Mawes. He heard later that some of the crew had been taken prisoner while others had been killed. The plane had been attacking the *Tusca Lusca* but the ship survived and was towed into harbour.

While he was in Cornwall, Harry heard that Alex Hamilton, a fellow evacuee who went to his school, had been killed by a bomb dropping on the house where he lived. Apparently, a metal gate was blown off its hinges and killed him. Luckily, his sister, Thelma, survived.

Mrs Jones remembers she was sixteen and certain units of the Army were recuperating in Falmouth after Dunkirk and they used to have some of the soldiers home for tea. A German plane swooped over their camp one day and bombed it. She could not believe that after all they had been through, this could happen. Falmouth and Plymouth were protected by pillar boxes, ack-ack batteries and barrage balloons, sited strategically both on ships and on shore. One of the RAF balloon detachments at Upton Mount consisted of ten men and women.

She was also in Truro with her mother collecting two evacuees off the train when a bomb fell on the hospital.

Mrs Jones suspected that the invasion of Europe was going to take place when she saw hundreds of American vehicles, filled with soldiers, just lazing around and some singing 'This is the Army, Mr Brown'. Suddenly, on 6 June they were gone; then she heard on the radio that the invasion had started.

Ken Foxon would sometimes lie awake and listen to the enemy planes going overhead. It was thought that they were after the gasworks. One morning when he woke up, he heard that German planes had machine gunned the streets of St Ives. Another night, a parachute mine caught on the side of a house and just hung there, swinging to and fro! Luckily, it did not go off before the bomb disposal unit disarmed it.

When Ken saw American troops scaling cliffs and training in St Ives he realized that the invasion of France was imminent. They had many accidents and a large number drowned when their floating tanks sank during rough weather.

One Saturday morning in 1944, Peter Butt was cleaning out the pig shed on Hillcrest Farm when he heard the droning sound of a bomber. He went outside and looked up, but could see nothing because of the low clouds. Suddenly, a twin-engine plane burst into sight over the top of Carn Brea, skimming over the main road, and landed in a field beyond. For a second, there was a deadly silence. An ear-splitting explosion suddenly filled the air as it burst into flames. Peter stood mesmerized, then across the fields he heard the fire engine bells ringing out as the emergency services made their way from Redruth. Later, Peter went back with his friend, John, to see if they could find any trophies but they could not get near the mangled metal because it was guarded. He will never forget that smell of burnt flesh.

Troops preparing for D-Day.

Peter got to know the driver of the milk lorry well and used to help him with the churns. One day, in January 1944, he was looking across the fields from Penzance Lane towards United Downs when he saw a large area of land being cleared and bell tents being erected. Soon, the tents were filled by thousands of American troops. The children would go to the camp and ask, 'Got any gum, chum?' They would also ask for lemonade crystals. Then, one day, Peter was returning from school and looked across at the camp and was surprised to see that the tents were empty and, within a week, they had all disappeared. It was as if the Americans had never been there.

One day, Brian Little and his twin brother were out in the fields at Baldu when they saw a low-flying German aircraft dropping bombs on the railway viaduct, but they missed. The plane then turned its attention to the people working in the fields and started machine gunning them. The brothers dived under the chicken sheds for cover. Later, they heard that a German plane had been shot down nearby and they both hoped it was the one that tried to kill them.

Mr Gill's son joined the Local Defence Volunteers, later know as the Home Guard. The LDV wore arm bands and Brian and his brother suggested the letters stood for 'Look, Duck and Vanish.'

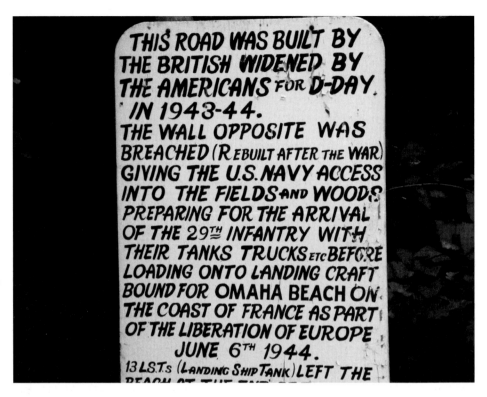

THIS ROAD WAS BUILT BY THE BRITISH WIDENED BY THE AMERICANS FOR D-DAY IN 1943-44. THE WALL OPPOSITE WAS BREACHED (Rebuilt after the war) GIVING THE U.S. NAVY ACCESS INTO THE FIELDS and WOODS PREPARING FOR THE ARRIVAL OF THE 29TH INFANTRY WITH THEIR TANKS TRUCKS etc BEFORE LOADING ONTO LANDING CRAFT BOUND FOR OMAHA BEACH ON THE COAST OF FRANCE AS PART OF THE LIBERATION OF EUROPE JUNE 6TH 1944. 13 L.S.Ts (Landing Ship Tank) LEFT THE

Plaque to commemorate the building of a road for the American 29th Infantry.

When the American troops arrived, Madeline Fereday (née Dunn) remembers everybody turning out and lining the streets, shouting and cheering their heads off as the lorries drove past. The vehicles were packed with troops and as they drove down the main street they threw out packets of sweets and gum. They were billeted on the Pendarves Estate and every night, Madeline and her sister would look out of their bedroom window and watch the soldiers cycle up to the fish and chip shop opposite. Madeline's father was a baker and if he was delivering to Penzance, Newquay or Porteath, where there was an American camp, he would take the girls with him. The Americans would give them gingerbread men, sweets and lollipops. The camp was highly secret because it was conducting gas experiments.

They did not have a shelter and during raids they would kneel under the stairs or dining table. Some of the local families had Anderson shelters in their gardens. One day, some men arrived and took away all the iron gates and railings from the village. She was puzzled as to why but found out later it was for the war effort, to make tanks, planes and shells.

Madeline's father was injured in the First World War and became a member of the Home Guard. He used to patrol each night, making sure people were not showing a light. He also kept a stirrup pump to put out local incendiary fires. When she went out after dark, she had to keep her torch shining down and remembers vehicles with slotted lights.

At night, as Madeline and her sister lay in bed and listened to the noise of the Germans flying overhead, they could see the night sky tinged with orange as bombs rained down on the docks at Falmouth and Plymouth. She saw Plymouth soon after the war and it was flattened but life went on, with shopkeepers selling from Nissen huts.

There was great excitement when a German plane was shot down just half a mile from where she lived and all the boys from the area converged on it for souvenirs. One boy was lucky enough to find a German helmet. All along the railway at Redruth, there were patrols. Sparks from the trains helped to guide enemy planes along the track and they would strafe them.

She remembers the Land Army girls working in the fields around the village and the dreaded telegraph boys with their red bikes and leather pouches. She can still hear the screams of mothers and sweethearts as they read the telegrams that told them that their loved ones were dead or missing.

Michael Duhig loved the military parades through the streets of Truro, when fighter planes would fly overhead. Often, Spitfires and Hurricanes would do a victory roll over the town, which made people feel good. In a field close to his house was a sandpit for putting out incendiary bombs, but the local children used to play in it. On one occasion while he was playing in it, he heard what sounded like a motorbike. When he looked, there was a German plane flying so low that Michael could see the pilot. They all ran for cover in case he started firing.

On his way to school one day Michael was surprised to see that all the local fields were crammed with tents, which were soon filled with American soldiers. The adults were not allowed on the camp but Michael and his gang used to roam through the camp unchallenged. They got to know some of the troops well and they would cadge chewing gum, lifesavers and anything that was going. In the middle of Truro there was an American canteen where they were given doughnuts.

One day, all the tents were empty and the few remaining sentries would not tell them where the soldiers had gone. Soon they learned the news of D-Day.

Madeline's brother-in law, John, remembers the American troops stationed at Nine Maiden. Some were black, which caused some racial problems between the troops.

While at Sunday school one day, he heard Spitfires come over and fly out to the coast and remembers machine gun fire and bombs dropping. There were gun emplacements all along the coast and rolls of barbed wire along the beaches with iron stakes driven in the sand at an angle, to prevent tanks rolling ashore. There appeared to be guns, searchlights and emergency vehicles everywhere. One Saturday morning, John heard the drone of an enemy plane and saw the Home Guard shooting at it with their rifles. At first he could not see it, then, suddenly, the clouds cleared and there it was, limping back to Germany.

One night, a plane was trying to bomb a train. Sir Arthur Carkeek, the famous engineer who built the Pendeen Lighthouse and many other buildings in Cornwall, was stood outside watching. Unfortunately, one of the bombs fell short and the blast killed him.

On another occasion, John was puzzled by a dark shadow which drifted across the fields before he realised it was a barrage balloon, trailing its rope behind it. Apparently, it had broken free from one of the ships in Falmouth harbour.

Madeline's cousin, Vera Andrewartha (née Bray), was eight years older than her and therefore remembers the evacuees. As a young woman she well remembers the American soldiers who were based in Troon. She, and her friend Mary, used to go dancing at the local church hall. Some of the Americans formed a Glen Miller band and they all danced to it. If she brought an American home, her mother used to give him supper. Her father had a greengrocery round with a horse and cart. At the end of the day he would finish up in the local pub. When he arrived home, many hours later, his cart would be full of Americans, who would stop for egg and chips. When the Americans moved out, Vera's mother received a letter from one of their wives thanking her for looking after her husband.

One night after Vera's father had finished his round, he put Nobby, the horse, out to graze and was sitting down for his evening meal when there was a loud crash. A bomb had dropped in one of his fields. He had a bad leg and could not walk very far, so Vera volunteered to look at the horse. Halfway across a field, she found her way barred by members of a searchlight party, who would not let her pass. She tried to explain why she had to go and finally persuaded them. Perhaps it helped that one of her elder sisters was going out with one of the group. She settled Nobby, who was trying to kick the door down. This was all done in the pitch dark and by a very young girl.

8

MISTREATMENT

My mother was fed up with living in the hotel. There were too many fights and quarrels. The women would stand there, toe to toe, pulling out handfuls of hair while others struggled to pull them apart. Mrs Parsons was a big woman and as strong as most men and broke up many a fight. When a fight broke out she would be there, holding back one of the combatants while two of the other ladies would hold back the other. The arguments were normally about children and while the mothers were fighting, the children who had caused the trouble would normally be making up behind their backs. Some of the fights were about men. Many of the women were going to the local dances to pick up soldiers and airmen who were far from home and lonely. When the Americans arrived, it was worse. With plenty of money and in their very smart uniforms, the women fell for them in droves.

I don't think that Mum went out with other men but I know that the next time my father came home, he suspected that she had. Somehow, Mum had a photograph of a soldier in her handbag and when my father went to her bag to get some change for his paper he found it. I don't know how it got there but at that time she never went out and left us, but I do remember lying on top of the cliffs while my brother and sister played while Mum talked to a Scotsman. My father went mad. It did not matter that he was going out and having a good time. It was evident in the letters Mum occasionally received from him that there was no real affection, and he seldom asked about us. They must have made it up though, for when he went back, she started getting fatter and I was not falling for that old chestnut that 'she was eating too much new bread.'

Nine months later Billy, Freddie and I finished up in the same home. This time they did not split us up but they still had the boring old jigsaw puzzle. To give them their due, they had added Snakes & Ladders and Ludo to their collection and Billy and I played for hours. When we got home we had our little sister, Violet, who, unlike Freddie, was as good as gold and rarely woke us up. It may have been the birth of Violet and the fact that we were getting very cramped in our one room that Mum decided to move to rooms in Mrs Turner's four-bedroom terraced house. Before the war, she did bed and breakfast for holidaymakers and now there were no holidaymakers, she took in evacuees, whom she loathed.

We were right at the top of the stairs and poor old Mum had to carry Violet up and down. She told us we had to be quieter than mice, which was asking the impossible of three boisterous boys. Mrs Turner hated us, and I am certain only tolerated us for the extra money we brought in. When Mum was not around, she would put her face next to mine and whisper, 'You are a horrible, dirty boy. I hope you die a horrible death.' I was terrified. I told Mum and she had words with Mrs Turner, who took no notice.

One day, Mum was out and I was in the kitchen, warming myself by a roaring fire while Mrs Turner ironed. In those days, most people did not have electric irons and would put a flat iron on the gas stove or on a metal stand on the fire. Suddenly, Mrs Turner glared at me and took the red-hot iron off the fire and turned, holding it inches from my face. I could feel the heat scorching me. At that moment, Mum came through the kitchen door and saw her. She snatched the iron and, holding it inches from Mrs Turner's face, screamed, 'How do you like it, you wicked cow?'

Mrs Turner, shrinking from Mum, screamed back, 'Get out of my house and take your brats with you!' And so we returned to the hotel where most of the women were pleased to see Mum. Some of them offered to go round and sort Mrs Turner out, but she would not hear of it.

—◦◦◦—

Although most people who had evacuees in their homes treated them well, there are many stories of mistreatment. Louise Willingham and her sister were evacuated during 1939, a few days before war was declared. They went with a number of other children and when they got off the train at Truro they were taken to a big hall. The two of them stood in a line, holding hands, while people came along and picked out the children they wanted. The sisters came from a very poor family and looked pretty scruffy. She thinks that is why they were not picked until almost last. An elderly lady rushed in at the last moment, just as they were wondering what was going to happen to them. She really did not have a lot of choice; it was the sisters or some scruffy-looking boy who kept cuffing his nose and another girl, Shirley. The old lady took the three girls. Perhaps she thought that the girls would be better at helping in the home. She might have thought all three were sisters, but they felt like Roman slaves being sold in a market place.

The old lady was very rough with the girls as she pushed them on a bus. They seemed to be travelling for hours, bearing in mind they had just come from London. Half asleep, they were pulled out of their seats and wearily walked up the long pathway, dragging their cases with two hands, stopping frequently. Before them was an old, dilapidated house. The red paint was flaking and the door had a hole in it for the letter box. As they got through the door the smell hit them, making them all feel sick. Next day, they found out why it smelt. It had been an old people's home but now it had only one resident, an old man who was incontinent. The poor old boy could not help it, but as children they did not understand.

They soon discovered that the toilet was right up the top of the garden in a wooden shed, full of spiders and without light. At night, they were terrified. If they wanted to go in the night, they would hold themselves until the morning. One night Shirley could not wait any longer. She had to go number two or bust. She took some newspaper and did it in that and wrapped it up and put it under the bed, meaning to dispose of it the following morning. The smell was terrible. Next morning Mrs Clifton came in and sniffed round the room, finally discovering the mess under the bed and roared in anger. For some unknown reason, she thought Louise had done it. She got hold of her by the hair and dragged her out of bed and into the passage. She paused at the top of the stairs and Louise looked down into the darkness below. The next moment, she was tumbling down. She thought she was going to die. She lay on the bottom step against the newel post. She thought she had broken every bone in her body as she tried to get up. Mrs Clifton flew down the stairs behind her and, grabbing her hair, pulled her to her feet and out of the door, where she discovered there were more steps as she was pushed head first. She was marched up the garden by her hair. She thought she was being scalped. At the end of the garden was the wooden toilet and she threw Louise in, screaming in her face, 'That's the place to go. If you ever do that again, I'll throw you down the hole!' Through her sobs, Louise whimpered, 'But it wasn't me ...' but Mrs Clifton would not listen.

One day, as a rare treat, Mrs Clifton took the three girls down to the beach. Louise wandered away and was looking in the rock pools when an old man came up to her and offered her a sweet if she would show him her sweetie. She screamed and Mrs Clifton came charging over but the old boy ran away.

As there was no bombing in London her father came down and took her back. She told her dad about the way Mrs Clifton had treated her and she thought he was going to have a row with her about it but, as he left, he just shook her hand and thanked her. Louise never forgave her father.

For reasons nobody explained to Frances Bishop and her two sisters, Joan and Pat, they were moved from billet to billet. In the first instance, they were moved from Mrs Wills' to live with a Mrs Treguna in Pool. She had a daughter called Jean who was the same age as Frances and they became close friends. Mr Treguna was a kind, gentle man who treated the sisters as if they were his own and his wife was just like her real mother who used to cut up old dresses and make the sisters and her daughter some beautiful clothes. She was so happy and then, one day, without warning, Frances was moved. She could not think why; she was devastated. After that, the only time she was happy was when she was at school. Soon after, her sister, Pat, joined her but they were badly neglected. The two sisters put up with it, never telling anybody. It was not done in those days; children should be seen but not heard. Nobody asked them how they were getting on or if they liked the place they were in. They felt completely on their own. The authorities just put them where they liked and the girls never questioned it, they just did as they were told.

There was another blow to come. One day, again without warning, they took Pat and put her with a lady in Barncoose Terrace. The lady's husband was a miner in South Africa and she lived alone. It was a good move for Pat and she was very happy there. She made friends with the family and eventually stayed. Frances was devastated. Without her sister she was alone, but she was happy for both her sisters because she learned that Joan was with a nice family called Greenslade. At least they were happy, even if she was not.

—⟡—

When we returned to the hotel, life went on as usual. Everybody took their turn in carrying out the different duties, which inevitably was a source of arguments, especially as some did not like the idea of working and would pay other women to do it. Where they got their money from one can only guess, but there were a lot of sex-starved soldiers about.

Most of the other hotels were taken over by the forces. A number catered for the wounded. I can remember seeing a pilot, which I knew by the wings on his chest, being pushed in a wheelchair by a friend. I was shocked by the burns on his face, but looked away because I did not want to embarrass him. That face brought the horror of war home to me, even at that young age.

Some of the hotels and halls held dances and a few of the women used to go. There was always someone like Mum who would baby-sit. At about one o'clock in the morning the whole hotel would be woken up as the women came back, dancing and singing along the corridors. They would come in and sit on the bed while Mum made them a drink. Frequently, they would fall asleep while sitting there. Mum would try to wake them up but if she could not they would lie there until the morning, when they would wake up and wonder where they were. Often, some of them would not come back all night. On occasions I heard Mum say things like, 'Jan is putting on weight, must be all that new bread she's eating. There'll be hell to pay when her old man finds out.' Although I did not say anything, I had leant that when Mum used the expression 'new bread' that there was a baby on the way and, sure enough, when Jan's husband came home after being wounded there was hell to pay!

He had been away for over a year and she was six months pregnant, or so I heard Mum say. The women seemed to come to Mum with their troubles; she was a very sympathetic person and, all her life, people told her their problems, although she had enough of her own. She had not heard from Dad for months and she was getting worried.

One day, Mum had a letter, and as she read it I could see it was bad news as her face went white and her hand shook. 'What's wrong, Mum? Is Dad alright?'

'It's your Uncle Bill; he's a prisoner of war in Germany.' Uncle Bill was my dad's brother, who I knew Mum liked, but I disliked him intensely. There was something about him. Before the war he had been a painter but during the recession of 1930 he, like millions of others, became unemployed and could not get a job, so he joined up and was in the 'Buffs', with whom he had been posted out to the Middle East. Despite my feelings about him, he was a brave, stubborn man. I learned when he came home that he had tried to escape eleven times and once, when he refused to go down the mines, the Germans threatened to shoot him. He never told of his experiences easily and normally had to be drunk before he did. We never heard from him again until the war was over and he turned up on Mum's doorstep, never to leave it until he died. Mum said, 'Your granddad was a prisoner of war in the First World War and was in Germany. He was alright, so perhaps Bill will be.'

I did hear the story of my grandfather's imprisonment and I think it saved his life when you think of the carnage of the First World War. He used to amuse me with his tale of when he worked on a German farm and a goat kept butting him up the backside. It did it once too often and he hit it on the head and killed it. The farmer thought it had died of natural causes and gave the carcass to him. He was starving and so, that night, he and his friends had full stomachs for once.

9

ENTERTAINMENT

Christmas was always great fun and although we had very few toys we all enjoyed ourselves. I remember the first Christmas we spent in Cornwall. The women made paper chains, which they strung across the dining hall. In the corner we had a large Christmas tree. I am not sure where they got the decorations from but it sparkled and had coloured lights. It has only recently occurred to me, after all these years, that the hotel must have lent them to us and I have no doubt that there were donations from some of the local shops. For weeks before, the women of the hotel saved up their rations for the day.

Before the big day, we were invited to one of the Army camps and sat in the big canteens on each side of a long line of trestle tables, which stretched the length of the room. There were evacuees from all over the local area. There must have been up to 100 children. We were fed sandwiches, cakes, jelly and ice cream until we nearly burst. I had never seen magic tricks before and I sat back spellbound as the magician first pulled handkerchiefs out of his sleeve, which seemed to go on and on. When he pulled a rabbit out of a hat, I was simply amazed. However, the best was yet to come. He asked for a volunteer and I rushed to the front, just beating one of the Snooty kids. The magician then began to pull half crowns from my ear. I could not believe it. He then showed me a box, which was empty, and I had to say the magic word, 'Abracadabra', as he tapped it with his wand. Then he rested the box on the table, turned it over and pulled three doves out, one after the other. They flew up into the roof and disappeared. He tapped the box again and out came more doves. That was real magic!

Then outside I heard the tinkle of sledge bells and, along with all the other children, I froze as I heard Father Christmas bellowing, 'Ho, ho, ho!' We stood up and screamed as this great figure came in with his red coat and flowing white beard. I must admit, I thought the beard was false and had lots of arguments with my friends who were convinced it was real. Over his shoulder he carried a great red sack. With a wave of his hands, he calmed us down and we waited with baited breath as a soldier beside him started calling out everyone's name. As my name came at the end of the alphabet, I wondered if there would be anything left for me as the sack became smaller and smaller. Would there be enough? Finally, my name was called and he handed me a tin fire engine. I was delighted.

The evacuees were very lucky and every camp in the surrounding area seemed to invite us to their party. Perhaps the soldiers and airmen were missing their own children, I do not know, but by the end of the Christmas period I must have put on a lot of weight. I longed for a box of soldiers and my father promised he would send some. On Christmas morning, I woke up long before Mum or the others and there at the bottom of the bed was a box. I could not contain myself and lay there for a while, thinking of the fun I would have. Finally, I could wait no longer. I reached out grasping the box. It seemed solid and I tore at the paper. I have never been so disappointed in my life; it was a box containing a pen and ink. My father had let me down again!

Once, he promised me a cricket set, not that I liked cricket, but in a letter to Mum he said he was going to send it to me and I told all my friends, even boasting to my enemies the Snootys. They questioned me closely, asking me if I was going to get pads; I did not even know what they were, let alone if I was going to get them. Week went on after week I waited for them to arrive and my friends kept saying, 'He's not going to send them. He's lying!' I defended my father as best I could by saying, 'They must have been lost in the post.' I had heard my mum say that when she did not receive something Dad promised. Needless to say, I never received them.

—◦◊◦—

John Glyn remembered two enjoyable Christmases in Newquay but returned to London as the bombing trailed off. He returned to his old school at White Hart Lane but, in 1944, he and the school were evacuated to Knaresborough in Yorkshire because of the new threat of V1 rockets. What was worse than them was the V2, which nobody could hear coming.

—◦◦◦—

The women from the hotel were invited to dances at many of the camps, which led to more affairs and divorces. Most of the women had boyfriends. When their husbands came home there were always rows, especially as some of the wives got pregnant or contracted VD – not that I would have known about such things in those days. There was one incident in which I have changed the names for obvious reasons, but I will call her Mrs Payne. I heard Mum whispering to Mrs Parsons, while they were doing their washing down in the basement, that Mrs Payne was seeing this bloke from the Army camp. She went on, 'I'm not saying too much as little piggies have big ears,' and she looked down at me. I pretended that I had not heard.

'What's he like?' asked Mrs Parsons. Apparently Mum had seen him once and thought he was good looking. Not that I was that interested, but all this talk of blokes and sex intrigued me. I wondered what it was all about.

—◦◦◦—

From the age of twelve, Patricia Free had taken tap dancing and acrobatic lessons in London and to her delight found a tap dancing classes in the local village, although she was well ahead of the class.

Nancy Botterell talks of how the older girls liked the American soldiers, with their smart uniforms and plenty of money. Her sisters went to local dances but her dad was always waiting at the gate to make sure they got home safely. The Yanks were camped on the Knaft, which was waste ground, and the favourite saying at that time was that 'The Yanks were overpaid, over-sexed and over here.'

Stan Mason was staying with the Laitys, who had a son about fifteen months older than him. They got on really well and would get up to mischief. One day, they got pulled up by the police for rolling round in the cornfields and destroying the crops, a criminal offence in those days. To supplement their diet Mr Laity used to catch rabbits and Stan was fascinated as he watched Mr Laity put his two ferrets down a rabbit hole and the rabbits ran out, straight into a net. There was also a stream at the bottom of the garden which contained eels and trout. One of them would pound the opposite bank with a pole to drive the fish into a net. Fish was a great change from rabbit.

The man in charge of the evacuees in Stan's area lived in a house in Constantine and he had an attractive daughter called Shirley, in whom Stan was rather interested. One day he was under a sycamore tree with her and bent across and kissed her. She was the first girl he kissed but, sadly, the relationship finished there and then!

Peter Butt had a treat nearly every Saturday because he was allowed to go to one of the two cinemas in Redruth, the Gem or the Regal. It seemed to him that the Gem showed cowboy and war films while the Regal had love stories; you can guess as a boy which one he liked the best! On top of that, when he came out of the cinema he would walk down the road to Morrish's fish and chip shop and enjoy the meal, washed down with a bottle of 'pop'.

Ken MacKinnon used to go to the local cinemas in St Ives. There were two of them and they would change their newsreel twice weekly, which kept him and everyone up to date with what was going on in the war. When anything came on to do with the Germans everybody booed, but when the British came on they cheered so much that there were fears for the roof. One newsreel, he remembers, showed British soldiers running around in the nude on some far-off beach. It drew shocked gasps from the audience. Often, while the film was showing the siren would go and everybody would rush out to the shelter.

One lady had a regular booking of a whole row of seats at the Scala cinema for her fourteen evacuees.

The lure of the Gaiety cinema in Newlyn was too much for Betty, Irene and Olive Hanton and they would walk the three miles there and back to see their favourite films and stars. By the time they got home they were tired, but they thought it was worth it. Sadly, the Gaiety is no more and has been turned into The Meadery restaurant. The girls also went to socials in the village hall and enjoyed jumble sales, Christmas parties and fêtes.

They were unable to go on most of the beaches and down to Lands End because there were rolls of barbed wire strewn across them. Instead, they used to go up to the Carne, which Betty describes as a wonderful high spot with rocks that was a lovely place for children to play.

All the evacuees and local children used to be invited to the American camp near Bodmin for parties. Shirley Downs remembers a large theatre that was on the American camp. All the children would sit in rows and were entertained by magicians and other acts. They were given sweets but her favourite were the doughnuts, with a hole in the middle and coated with sugar. She had never seen anything like it before.

As children they had also never seen a black person before and it came as a surprise when they opened their front door and found one sitting on the front step. He had stopped to ask for water.

Mrs Jones (née Mitchell) was a young woman and loved to go to the dances in the wooden hall at Perranporth, which were run by the Women's Institute. There were lots of soldiers, all in uniform, most in boots. If any took her home her father would be waiting at the door to make sure she was safe. At one of the dances, she met her future husband. Her father and mother would sometimes have soldiers home to tea.

Mary Garnham remembers the euphoria of VE Day. Everybody was grinning and hugging one another and the church bells rang for the first time since the war started. Street parties were held with trestle tables that spanned the street, laden with everything people could spare (there was still rationing), including

From left to right, back row: Rose Plant, Maureen Wherry. Front row: Rose Rumball, Mary Garnham (née Rumball), Cyril Rumball, Irene Rumball.

sandwiches, cakes, jellies and orange drinks. Music blared out from houses that had a gramophone and it seemed to be in stereo as it came from both sides of the street. People were jitterbugging in the road and the parties went on all night and, in some cases, continued into the next day.

On VE Day in St Just there were a number of parties, and Sheila Nicholas had all she could eat; jellies, cakes and ice cream. The soldiers also arranged a marionette show and she was enthralled by the magic of the puppets. At the end of the show, as they trooped out of the hall, a man handed them a threepence piece, which was a fortune in those days. Unfortunately, she cannot remember how she spent it.

During the weekdays, after school, Eileen Penwarden played games with her friends. They all loved to go down to the harbour at Mevagissey and play on the beach. At weekends, she and her friends would pack a picnic and go further afield to the remote Chapel Point, where they would wade in the stream that ran down to the sea and pick watercress.

At Christmas, and occasionally at other times during the year, concerts were held in the village hall and the soldiers took part. A lot of the girls had a crush on one of the soldiers who was good looking and had a wonderful voice. Her mum and dad came down after the bombing had stopped and took her home for Christmas and she never went back, despite the doodlebugs and V2 rockets.

Children made their own entertainment in those days. Of course, there was the cinema, but few could afford to go often. The radio, apart from *Children's Hour*, catered mainly for adults and so children like Jean Pickering played games such as rounders, climbed trees and made go carts out of old bits of wood and old wheels. The carts would be steered by a piece of rope tied to both sides of the front axle. The carts were very difficult to control when going downhill and many a prize rose got flattened. Some children made scooters out of two planks of wood, one for standing on while the other was upright and was attached to it by a bolt. The wheels, if you could get them, were old ball bearings. The only problem was that the ball bearings made a terrible noise on the roads, but at least there were not many cars.

The sea was always a great adventure and provided hours of entertainment, especially for those who could swim. Ian Blackwell and his sister, Heather, were strong swimmers and he would swim out about half a mile but his sister, being a better swimmer, would swim on to try to reach the dolphins so that she could swim with them. They would also climb rocks, sometimes to find sea gulls' eggs. One evening, Ian climbed down Dodman Point, which he believes is the highest headland on the south Cornish coast.

Inevitably, as the evacuees became teenagers, they formed relationships with girls and Ian remembers wandering down to the deserted beach with a girl called Joyce and sitting and talking to her for ages. When it rained, they would go to a shed where there was a cart loaded with hay and would just sit and talk. He also remembers his first kiss and he had to stand on a step to reach her lips because she was taller than him.

When peace was announced, Madeline Fereday was at school in Troon. The headmaster, cheering, led the pupils and teachers outside, where everybody paraded through the streets waving flags. Soon, all the villagers came out and stood cheering at the side of the road, ecstatic that the fighting was over and that we had won.

10

RETURNING HOME

When the evacuees returned home, be it after the Blitz or when the war finished, everything had changed. It was a different world. Those who had lived on great, spreading farms were astonished how small their own homes were and, for a time, some found it claustrophobic. Complete streets had been razed to the ground. Houses had no roofs and the rafters were left exposed, pointing to the sky.

———— ∽∽∽ ————

Our house had been completely destroyed by a landmine a fortnight after we were evacuated to Cornwall. During the latter part of the war, we went to live with our grandparents in Essex because my grandmother was ill. One day, we had a surprise visit from Uncle Bill, who looked pale and haggard after being released from a German prisoner of war camp. My parents were divorcing and Mum began to see more and more of Uncle Bill. At the same time, my Uncle Jim came home after having been fighting with the 'Desert Rats'. He was bronzed, tall and so thin I hardly recognised him.

My grandmother began to recover and so Mum started to look for somewhere to live. She applied to Hackney Borough Council and soon we were allocated a prefab in Haggerston Road; Uncle Bill, my father's brother, moved in with us. In view of the number of properties destroyed, Churchill introduced the Temporary Housing Programme in 1945. The prefabs were mass-produced and 156,600 were built. They were wonderful and Mum was in heaven. They had two bedrooms, a living room, a fitted kitchen, bathroom, refrigerator and coal back-boiler. It was far superior to our old house. There was, however, a major problem of bugs and to overcome this, the council baked everybody's furniture, no matter whose.

Behind our prefab was a bomb-site where we used to have bonfires and cook potatoes. There seemed to be a large number of bent metal sheets, which we used to see-saw on and build camps. We went into bombed-out houses and swung and balanced across floor joists two floors up.

Street parties for VE day were held in the roads and trestle tables were put up all along the street. We all wore paper Union Jack hats. Bunting was strung across the streets. One of the neighbours brought out their piano and thumped out all the old songs long into the night. Lemonade for the children and beer for the grown-ups flowed like water. I have never been so full in my life. I cannot remember going to bed that night but when I woke in the morning, I was fully dressed.

———✦———

When her mother took her home after the Blitz appeared to have finished in 1942, Jean Pickering felt her house seemed so small. Towards the end of the war there were the doodlebugs and V2s. Everybody got used to the sound of the doodlebugs coming over. At the distinctive noise of their engines, people would stop and stare up into the skies, hoping that the engine would not cut out. When it did, they would throw themselves on the ground and pray. Jean was in the cinema one day and through the walls she could hear the drone of

Street parties like this were held all over the country.

125

a doodlebug. The audience waited with baited breath and gave a sigh of relief when they heard the explosion elsewhere.

The V2 rockets were far worse because you never heard them coming. One day, Jean was looking up from the garden while speaking to her mother through a window, when suddenly, there was a loud explosion and glass from every window was shattered. She could not believe that she and her mother had escaped injury. One of her uncles was badly injured by a rocket, which fell just outside his house. He was in bed at the time and he was lifted, bed and all, as far as the back garden. The attacks got so bad that she was evacuated again, this time to Corton Holiday Camp, near Lowestoft.

At the end of the war Betty Hanton decided that because she had enjoyed her time on the farm so much she would join the Land Army, but only got as far as Wiltshire, where she met her future husband.

Edna Goreing remembers the street party for VE Day. The King and Queen came down and she watched them from the window of her house as the soldiers marched past. She particularly remembers the Americans, who made a deep impression on her in their smart uniforms and playing jazz. After the parade she strutted around for days pretending to be the Queen.

Michael Duhig was at school when he heard that the war was over and, to celebrate, they were all sent home early. When he got home he found Mrs Hubber was crying and realised later that it was not because the war was over, but that it meant he would be going back to London. The morning he left, in June 1945, Mr Hubber took him to the station in a taxi while Mrs Hubber stood at the door crying her eyes out. As the train pulled out of the station, he noticed that Mr Hubber was crying. At first, Michael did not think it affected him until he got home and realised that his own family were strangers, and he broke down and cried. It took some years to get over it.

Everybody thought that the danger in London had passed and some evacuees began to drift back home. Ian Blackwell's parents were no exception and wanted him and his sister, Heather, back with them. Sadly, and for the last time, he took his girlfriend, Joyce, up the lane to a gate which looked out on Dodman Point. The sun was setting in a golden haze and Joyce turned to Ian and said, 'Remember this.' Joyce's words reflect what most evacuees felt on returning home:

We will remember those far-off days of sunshine and sand, and the kindness, love and understanding that most Cornish people gave us evacuees during the time they sheltered us in their homes, and with one voice, we say, 'Thank you!'

Left: *The Evacuees Reunion Association flag at St Paul's. The standard bearer, Reg Baker, is assisted by the author.*

Below: *St Paul's on the seventieth anniversary.*

Other titles published by The History Press

A Schoolboy's War in Essex
DAVID F. WOOD

David F. Wood recalls his days as a schoolboy in Essex, where his family moved when the Luftwaffe threatened his native London. With the same sense of fascination that grips many men of his generation, he describes watching airmen parachute to safety during the Battle of Britain and witnessing a Messerschmitt dramatically crash-landing close to his home. The accounts of his days spent playing with his new friends in the nearby countryside provide a stark contrast to the ravages of a war that was going on all around them.

978 0 7524 5517 4

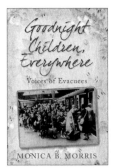

Goodnight Children, Everywhere
MONICA B. MORRIS

For the many children torn from their families, taken miles from home and placed with strangers, the evacuation at the outbreak of the Second World War was a life-changing experience. In *Goodnight Children, Everywhere*, men and women who were children at the time recall their poignant memories of being labelled, lined up and taken away. Some children were advantaged by the dramatic change in their lives; others, separated from all they knew and loved, suffered unendurable heartbreak. This is their story.

978 0 7524 5282 1

Liverpool's Children in the Second World War
PAMELA RUSSELL

This is the untold story of Liverpool's children in the Second World War. Whilst everyone is familiar with the tales of evacuees who were rushed out of the cities once the bombs started falling, many of us are unaware that many stayed behind, either by choice or necessity, as the city of their childhood disintegrated and burned around them. Ideal for anyone who is fascinated by experiences and the legacy of the wartime generation, this title pays tribute to the war's forgotten children.

978 0 7524 5158 9

Cornwall at War
ELIZABETH HOTTEN

Covering the Boer, First and Second World Wars, this fascinating book reproduces letters and articles published in parish magazines from across Cornwall between 1889 and 1951. News travelled slowly, so letters sent home were considered interesting and informative to both loved ones and the local community. The majority of letters were written by officers to their families, and provide a rare insight into conditions on the front line when official news was scarce and often out of date.

978 0 7509 5097 8

Visit our website and discover thousands of other History Press books.

www.thehistorypress.co.uk